Embracing Hopelessness

Embracing Hopelessness

Miguel A. De La Torre

Fortress Press
Minneapolis

EMBRACING HOPELESSNESS

Cover image: Thinkstock: 126401302/sodapix sodapix/-

Cover design: Lauren Osman

Print ISBN: 978-1-5064-3341-7

eBook ISBN: 978-1-5064-3342-4

The paper used in this publication meets the minimum requirements of American
National Standard for Information Sciences — Permanence of Paper for Printed
Library Materials, ANSI Z329.48-1984.

Manufactured in the U.S.A.

This book was produced using Pressbooks.com, and PDF rendering was done by
PrinceXML.

TO:

Tink

in celebration of his 2018 retirement
and the decades of shaping minds
including this author's

Contents

Acknowledgments

In an earlier book (*The U.S. Immigration Crisis: Toward an Ethics of Place*), I made an argument for an ethics of place, a perspective influenced by Clodovis Boff's five-month missionary journey through the remote jungles of Western Brazil. His book *Feet-on-the-Ground Theology* records conversation with the rubber gatherers he encounters while ministering to their needs. To do theological reflection requires sharing in the lives, the hardships, the pain, and the concerns of those forced to exist on the margins of power and privilege. To engage in liberative ethical analysis requires accompanying the oppressed in their struggles; leaving the safety of ivory towers to occupy precarious spaces alongside the disenfranchised. In short, one must be *¡Presente!* To be present moves away from theorizing about the oppressed as if they are simply some object upon which to gaze. An ethics of place[1] recognizes the physical location where the oppressed reside as being crucial in understanding which ethics, which praxis, needs to be engaged. Not to be *presente* questions the ability to truly comprehend the dilemma under investigation. Physically engaging in consciousness-raising praxis provides a better understanding concerning the causes of oppression and how they are manifested in the everyday, facilitating

---

1. I am aware that scholars such as Mick Smith have used the term "ethics of place" as a means by which to reengage the moral and ethical concerns of radical ecological theories; that J. K. Gibson Graham uses the term "ethics of the local" in a Marxist analysis grounded in the necessary failure of the global order; and that John Inge uses the term "theology of place" to stress taking seriously the importance of place and how it contributes to the creation of the identity of community and vice versa, with both endangered by the effects of globalization responsible for the erosion of people's rootedness. I am using the phrase "ethics of place" somewhat differently than how others have used the term. For me, an ethics of place means praxis must be developed in the place of oppression, in the midst of the effects of institutionalized disenfranchisement, in the hope of creating an ethical response. When I use the term "ethics of place," I mean that ethical analysis, to be contextual, must also pay close attention to the physical locale of the marginalized.

better-informed theories or doctrines. In the doing of liberative acts (ethics), theory (theology) is formed as a reflection of praxis.

To that end, I made it a point to physically go to where oppression has and/or continues to exist. In reality, I could have picked any number of atrocities where everyday lives have been crushed under the grindstone of history: child soldiers, the US gun epidemic, sex trafficking, clergy rape of children. Locales and topics chosen were, to some extent, arbitrary. Realizing that a multiple number of atrocities exist from which to bear testimony to the hopelessness of human existence, I did not visit these randomly chosen locales of oppression solo. I asked fellow scholars to accompany me in my journey with their conversation and insight. Because the focus of my research (unlike the previous two books in this trilogy) moves beyond the US Latinx experience, I initiated conversations with individuals of different races, ethnicities, and religious persuasions. And while my focus remains rooted in my own Christian faith, I reached out to non-Christians to hold me accountable, in an attempt to safeguard me from normalizing my reality. As I was writing each chapter, I was in dialogue with my conversation partner, and upon completing the chapter, I shared my writing to obtain additional insights, critiques, and feedback. In a very real way, this book is a product of what Latinx scholars call a *teología de conjunto* (also known as a *teología en conjunto*).

The term *teología de conjunto* translates as doing theology in conjunction, or jointly. To engage in a *teología de conjunto* is to employ a communal methodology of theorizing characteristic of the US Latinx theological movement. This approach originates in and reflects upon the lived reality of marginalized communities and involves a process by which scholars, ministers, and laypersons gather and reflect together. But if truth be known, all too often Latinx scholars edit an anthology by asking different scholars to write individual chapters, seldom discussing their thoughts and writings, and having minimal connection to others writing their own individual chapters for the same volume. Few actually take the time to engage and wrestle with each other's thoughts when theorizing theological and ethical concepts. All too often, the only difference between a Latinx-edited book and a Eurocentric-edited book is that the former refers to their edited volume as a *teología de conjunto*. But a *teología de conjunto* must mean more than what Euroamericans also do; it must encompass the give-and-take of discourse during the writing project. The methodology employed in writing this particular book was an attempt to capture the spirit of what Latinx originally meant by the term *teología de conjunto*, while expanding the Latinx-centric methodology to include those of different ethnic, racial, and religious traditions. To that end, I am deeply grateful to the following scholars for agreeing to challenge my thinking and be my conversation partners:

Chapter 1 – Grace Ji-Sun Kim, a Korean Christian

Chapter 2 – George "Tink" Tinker, a Native American

Chapters 1 & 2 – Albert Hernández, a Latinx historian

Chapter 3 – Santiago Slabodsky, a Latin American Jew

Chapter 4 – Stacey Floyd-Thomas, a womanist

Chapter 5 – John Fife, a Euroamerican Christian minister.

To all of them, who made this final book of my trilogy possible: *¡Muchisima Gracias!*

Preface: The Order of Things

For the traditionalist thinker, this book might very well be considered the first of a trilogy, even though the other two books have already been published. But those who engage in liberative ethics will have no difficulty in seeing this book as the third and final installment. In *Latina/o Social Ethics: Moving Beyond Eurocentric Moral Thinking* (Baylor University Press, 2010), I focused on praxis, the doing of ethics; while in *The Politics of Jesús* (Rowman & Littlefield, 2015), I explored the biblical text to understand the praxis advocated in the first book. In this third book, I turn to theological and theoretical understandings based on the praxis employed in the first book and the biblical witness given by the second book. Hence, the correct order of things: from action flows understanding. This methodology differs radically from the way Eurocentric thought has been constructed: normativity conducted deductively. From some theology or theory (or truth) comes the action (or praxis) done to remain faithful to what is already believed and decided. First comes some conceptualized universal truth, such as an ideology, a philosophy, a biblical interpretation, or a church teaching. Then, based on this truth, an action—as a second step to life—is determined and implemented. Orthopraxis, as this formula goes, flows from orthodoxy. If I was to follow this normative methodology, then this book—which focuses on the theoretical—should have come first, followed by *The Politics of Jesús* (an attempt to biblically justify what we decided to do), and finally *Latina/o Social Ethics* (actions in which to engage). Liberative[1]

1. In my 2008 book, *The Hope of Liberation within World Religions* (Baylor University Press), I moved away from the term "liberationist ethics," arguing that while liberationist is a type of liberative ethics, liberative ethics is not necessarily liberationist. Liberation ethics has historically been based on liberation theology (usually rooted in 1960s Latin America), which is characteristically Christian (predominately Catholic). Liberative ethics, like liberation theology, still emphasizes the preferential option for the oppressed, but in doing so, might—but will not necessarily—center its

ethicists, however, turn this methodology upon its head, arguing theology is the second step, where orthodoxy instead flows from orthopraxis. Truth, beyond the historical experiences and the social location where individuals act as social agents, cannot be ascertained, whether said truth exists or not. Only through justice-based praxis, engaged in transforming society, can individuals come closer to understanding the spiritual and theoretical. For this reason, the praxis focus book *Latina/o Social Ethics* came first. That particular book ended by emphasizing the importance of Jesus Christ for a Christian-based ethics, hence the second book *The Politics of Jesús*, which in turn ends on a hopeless note—the focus of this book.

In the proper order of things, this book explores what it means to move away from a middle-class privilege, which assumes all is going to work out in the end. All things, in spite of Romans 8:28, do not always work for good for those called by God's purposes. For those of us who choose to sit in solidarity with Job, a man who loved God, we deal with an existing hopelessness regardless of the faithfulness of the one being crushed. After all, the text reminds us that a more faithful servant did not exist. And yet, on a dare from Satan who proposed that Job would curse and reject God if God visited calamity upon him rather than blessings, God took away his wealth, slaughtered his children, and afflicted his health. When Job looks to the Heavens for an answer, he receives a troubling response from God. Tough sh*t—I am God and I do whatever I want. The God of Job reminds us how precarious life is, regardless of faith in or allegiance to the Almighty. The faithful of the world, especially those relegated to the underside of white and class privilege, have little hope of resolution to the hopeless situation in which they find themselves. The piles of innocent corpses littering history testify to the bankruptcy of any type of dialectical or salvation history ushering some utopia.

This book may be as hard to read as it has been to write. After all, the very foundation of God's spiritual gifts, claimed by followers of Christ, is love, joy, peace, and hope; and I have the audacity to argue that hope, as an illusion, is responsible for maintaining oppressive structures? In a very real sense, like Jacob the patriarch, this book and I grapple with a God who refuses to show God's face (Gen 32:24–32). We live in a world where evil prevails. Oppression, abuse, and violence are more the norm

reasoning on Christian concepts. The focus of liberative ethics moves away from orthodoxy, correct doctrine, toward orthopraxis, the correct actions required to bring about liberation. So while liberationism is Christian, liberative ethics can be Muslim, Hindu, humanist, or Buddhist.

(more so when perpetrated by those professing to be Christians) than the love, joy, peace, and hope promised in Holy Writ. Just as Jacob wrestles to see God's face, so too do this book and I wrestle to see the face of a seemingly absent God in the midst of a suffering world; a world where premature death and marginalization are more common than things working for good for those who are called according to God's purposes. This book struggles with a God who at times seems mute, demanding solidarity in the midst of perdition and a blessing in the midst of adversity. How can the Creator be so invisible during the troubling times in which we live—times filled with unbearable life-denying trials and tribulations? Jacob wrestles with God, demanding to be given a blessing; but we must wonder if there even is a God with whom to wrestle.

Fighting God to see God face-to-face has consequences. Not only does the ordeal make Jacob a new person, being called Israel from that day forward, but he also limps away—an injury to constantly remind him, for the rest of his days, of his encounter with the Divine. Likewise, there are consequences (at least for me as the author of this book) to truly engage in a spiritual brawl, struggling to see the face of God that circumstances make hard to believe in. Like Jacob, I might receive a blessing, but usually it comes at a cost. I want to believe, and find myself holding on to faith—if only by my fingertips. I enter this wrestling match with the Almighty, hoping against hope to be renewed, for faith has proven powerful in transforming lives throughout the ages. Ideally, the transformation is for the better, but history has shown us this is not always the case.

Introduction

"Vanity of vanities," laments the author of Ecclesiastes. "Absolute futility. Everything is meaningless" (Eccles 1:1). All is pointless, the teacher reminds us, a chasing after wind (2:17). Humanity's fate is no different from animals: both die and go to the same place. All that lives comes from dust and to dust all that lives returns (3:19–20). When the writer of Ecclesiastes contemplates the oppression taking place under the sun, the author concludes:

> I gazed upon the tears of the oppressed,
> and they have no one to comfort them;
> power resides with their oppressors,
> and they have no one to comfort them.
> I proclaim the dead,
> those who have died,
> are happier than the living
> those who are still alive.
> Better still than both
> is the one never born
> whose eyes have not witnessed evil
> done under the sun. (4:1–3)[1]

If I could succinctly paraphrase this passage of Scripture, it would be: Sh*t happens. We live in an era where a people are divided by a demilitarized zone that separates families and loved ones, and constantly live under the threat of war and violence. We live with the consequences of past massacres when a primitive and savage people commit genocide on an indigenous population. The post-traumatic stress

---

1. Unless otherwise noted, all biblical quotationss were translated by the author from the original language.

1

of a people, caused by centuries of bloodletting, is genetically passed down from generation to generation, funneling many to the poorest and most underserved lands within the nation. A more recent mass genocide, perpetrated with mechanized efficiency, has not tempered anti-Semitic sentiments, and hatred for the religious Other takes new forms, as in the case of Islamophobia. And finally, black lives continue not to matter—nor do brown lives. We live under a constructed history perpetuating a false justification of oppressive structures geared on privileging one group over against others. In the midst of overlapping unjust structures and the intersection of racism, classism, ethnic discrimination, sexism, heterosexism, and all the other ideologically based "isms" imaginable, a sense of hopelessness grips the soul as realization of the depths of oppression makes solutions appear simplistic. Better not to have been born is the comfort Holy Scripture offers.

But even if we were to find a path diminishing the structural oppressions of our time, and took steps toward restitution, we would still maintain a neoliberal global structure responsible for much of the world's misery. Of the seven billion earth inhabitants in 2010, 1.75 billion in 104 countries (about a third of their population) lived in multidimensional poverty, reflecting acute deprivation in health, education, and standard of living (UNDP 2010: 78, 80, 96). Dire economic situations are not limited to the two-third world. Even within the richest nation ever known to humanity, the gap in income and wealth is greater now than ever in recent history. The US poverty rate in 2010 was 15.1 percent, with 46.2 million people (the largest number in fifty-two years) living in poverty (DeNavas-Walt et al. 2011: 5).[2] Because the 1 percent controls the vast majority of the wealth, by extension, they also control the political systems that protect their riches, thus making the hope of bringing about a more just distribution of wealth futile.

But even if we develop new economical models while averting bloodshed, we still are rushing toward an environmental holocaust that could render our planet uninhabitable. Although a small conservative Christian segment of the American population dismisses global warming as a hoax, the first six months of 2012 were the hottest in the US since record keeping began in 1895, as the US experienced the worst drought in fifty-six years (Glenn, Gordon, and Florescu 2012: 3). The United Nations has estimated that by 2050, the adverse impact of cli-

2. Lynnley Browning, "U.S. Income Gap Widening, Study Says," *The New York Times*, September 25, 2003; and Binyamin Appelbaum, "For U.S. Families, Net Worth Falls to 1990s Levels," *The New York Times*, June 12, 2012.

mate change on grain yields will double the price of wheat, leaving 25 million additional children malnourished (UNDP 2010: 102). An eighteen-month 2012 study commissioned by the Central Intelligence Agency concluded that climate-driven crises could lead to domestic instability or international crises in food markets, water supplies, energy supplies, and public health systems.[3] In response to the overwhelming evidence of global warming, upon which climate scientists are in agreement, the world's richest nations are spending billions to limit their own risks from global warming's consequences, specifically rising sea levels and drought.

And yet the industrial North, which is responsible for most of the global warming, will be affected least. Continents like Africa, which accounts for less than 3 percent of the global emissions of carbon dioxide from fuel burning since 1900, face the greatest risks caused by drought and the disruption of water supplies.[4] The poorest 40 percent of the world's population, some 2.6 billion people, will experience "a future of diminished opportunity" as they bear the brunt of climate change (UNDP 2007: 2). Regardless of the good intentions of those who are privileged by society, or the praxis they employ to paternalistically save the world's marginalized, the devastating consequences of neoliberalism and climate change will worsen as the few get wealthier and the many sink deeper into the despair of stomach-wrenching poverty. Those with power, including progressives, may be willing to offer charity and to stand in solidarity, but few are willing or able to take a role in dismantling the global structures designed to privilege them at the expense of others.

But even if the earth's inhabitants bond together to address our common environmental threat and avoid being the cause of our own extinction, the cosmos continues to conspire against us. Human extinction is inevitable, either by an asteroid similar to the one that eradicated the dinosaurs, or some black hole. And even if we escape the mathematical probabilities of such random astrological events, we still cannot escape the hopelessness of the human dilemma. Our sun, like all other stars in the universe, will one day expand to become a red giant, bringing an end to all that lives. "Vanity of vanities, absolute futility. Everything is meaningless."

The author of Ecclesiastes captures the futility of human existence:

---

3. John M. Broder, "Report Outlines Climate Change Perils," *The New York Times*, November 10, 2012.
4. Andrew C. Revkin, "Poorest Nations Will Bear Brunt as World Warms," *The New York Times*, April 1, 2007.

"At least the living know they will die, the dead know nothing. No more reward for them, their memory is forgotten" (8:5). In a pre-Internet age, we forgot those who preceded us as completely as those who post-dated us would have forgotten us. We may believe, in this digital age, that our electronic footprint will remain long after we are nothing but food for worms, but if humanity itself comes to an end, there will be no one to remember us under the sun—if even a sun exists.

So, are the nontheists right? There is no God, so why bother with religiosity? I certainly do not need the arguments of the atheists to convince me not to believe; I just need to witness the actions of those who claim to believe—e.g., Christians who led the crusades, the inquisition, and the conquest of Others in the name of Jesus. If I simply concentrate on U.S. history, Christians are behind all of this nation's atrocities—the genocide of the indigenous people to steal their land, the enslavement of Africans to work the stolen land, and the stealing of cheap labor and natural resources of Latin Americans under the guise of "gunboat diplomacy" to develop the land. All these atrocities, along with more than can be listed here, were conducted with Christian justification. The support for racist and misogynist politicians by so-called evangelicals during the 2016 presidential election reinforces the fact that Christians have continually stood on the wrong side of history. All too often, I believe, nontheists are closer to God than Christians. How then does one hope in the face of nihilism? In the face of a God used by the faithful to justify barbarisms? How does one hold on to faith, even if it's by one's fingertips? Avoiding the ostrich response of sticking one's head in the sand and ignoring reality by continuing to recite Romans 8:28, in this book I will attempt to explore faith-based responses to unending injustices by embracing the reality of hopelessness. This book rejects the pontifications of a salvation history that moves the faithful toward an eschatological promise which, looking back at history, tries to make sense of all Christian-led brutalities, mayhem, and carnage.

For so many of the world's disenfranchised, they occupy the space of Holy Saturday—the day after Good Friday's crucifixion—and the not-yet Easter Sunday of resurrection. This is a space where the faint anticipation of Sunday's Good News is easily drowned out by the reality and consequences of Friday's violence and brutality. It is a space where hopelessness becomes the companion of those who are used and abused. The virtue and/or audacity of hope becomes a class privilege experienced by those protected from the realities of Friday or the opium used by the poor to numb that same reality until Sunday rolls around. Regardless of the optimism professed, the disenfranchised, their children, and their children's children will more than likely continue to live in an ever-expanding poverty necessary for the benefit of the empire's center. Sunday seems so far away. The situation, regardless of the skin pigmentation or gender of whoever the president of the empire happens to be, remains hopeless.

I first began to develop a theology of hopelessness in 2006 when I took a group of predominately white students to the squatter villages of Cuernavaca, Mexico to learn from the poor. During our outing we spoke with many families living in horrific conditions. That evening, as we processed the day's activities, one student struggling with what she had witnessed shared that in spite of the miserable conditions in which these people lived, she still saw "hope in the eyes of the little girls." Hope, as a middle-class privilege, soothes the conscience of those complicit with oppressive structures, lulling them to do nothing except look forward to a salvific future where every wrong will be righted and every tear wiped away, while numbing themselves to the pain of those oppressed, lest that pain motivate them to take radical action. Hope is possible when privilege allows for a future. A child can hope when college is assured, when parents know how to game the system to advance themselves and their progeny economically, when safety and lack of fear create a livable environment. Even the hopeless can be distracted when stomachs are filled and rest can be found in warm comfortable beds. But for so many from minoritized communities where surviving into adulthood is itself a challenge, and where skin pigmentation ensures lack of opportunities to wealth and health, hope runs in short supply. My immediate response was to explain that this same little girl in whose eyes my student saw hope would more than likely be selling her body in a few years to put food on the table or would be trapped in an abusive marriage attempting to survive classism and sexism, so I wasn't sure what kind of hope my student detected. Among the disenfranchised, the dispossessed, the least of the least, I discovered an ethos where hope is not apparent; rather, it is imposed by those who might be endangered if the marginalized were to instead act.

Since that encounter, I have been wrestling with the realization that for many of the ultra-poor, hope seems to be mainly claimed by those with economic privilege as a means of distancing themselves from the unsolvable disenfranchisement most of the world's wretched are forced to face. *The first step toward liberation requires the crucifixion of hope*—for as long as hope exists, the world's wretched have something to lose, and thus will not risk all to change the social structures. The realization that there is nothing to lose becomes a catalyst for praxis. I argue that by embracing hopelessness, a peace surpassing all understanding will equip us to engage in radical praxis that might make our short and brutal days upon this earth a bit more just. So, what is this hopelessness that I call us to embrace? Through an analysis of the intersection of power (specifically the colonization of the mind) and truth (as defined by those with the power and privilege to construct the official history), this book attempts to dislocate the religious meaning of hope responsible for sustaining and maintaining an oppressive status quo. I am less interested in how hope contributes to religious belief than I am in the function of hope in reinforcing oppressive structures and reining in revolutionary tendencies. To this task, we now turn our attention.

1

Those Who Ignore History Are Condemned to Construct New Ones

Standing on a windy hilltop, some thirty-five miles north of Seoul, I gazed northward toward North Korea, overlooking the city of Kijong-dong. When the 1953 armistice was signed, bringing a precarious and continuous ceasefire to the Korean War (1950–53), a two-and-a-half-mile-wide demilitarized zone (DMZ) was established, snaking along the thirty-eighth parallel for 151 miles across the Korean Peninsula's waistline. Within this no-man's-land littered with some two million land mines (my military escort joked about the numerous three-legged boars), are two towns sitting about a mile opposite each other. These are the only inhabited towns located within the DMZ. Separated by the Seocheongang River, a small bridge—the Bridge of No Return—serves as the only ground link between the two towns and two countries. Since the armistice, this is the locale where prisoners of war are repatriated.

In the south there is a small farming village of about 225 residents called Daeseong-dong, which translates as "Attaining Success Village," better known as "Freedom Village." To the north lies Kijong-dong, which can be translated as Peace Village; although the US military personnel patrolling the DMZ refers to it as "Propaganda Village."

Whether it be Attaining Success Village, or Peace Village, both towns, in reality, are Propaganda Villages. Kijong-dong, which appears luxurious from the distant hilltop where I stand, is committed to peace. The city boasts that none of its inhabitants have ever fought in a war, shot a weapon, or committed any harm toward another human being. This amazing feat is possible because no one lives in this Potemkin village, even though North Korea insists that over 200 families call Kijong-dong home.

As I look through my binoculars toward Kijong-dong, I experience an eerie sensation similar to some *Twilight Zone* episode, of witnessing a well-manicured and -maintained ghost town devoid of human life. The multistory, brightly painted buildings are shells, absent of glass in their windows and subdivided interior rooms. Electric lights (a luxury in rural North Korea) are placed on automatic timers to flicker on during the night, giving the illusion of habitation. About fifteen to twenty maintenance workers are tasked with ensuring the illusion is maintained. On certain days, they can be seen sweeping empty streets.

In the center of the town, overshadowing the façades, is a humongous flagpole upon which a six-hundred-pound North Korean flag proudly waves. In 1980, when the South Korean town of Daeseong-dong raised a 323-foot flagpole upon which to wave its flag, the North Koreans, not to be outdone (pole envy?), raised a 525-foot flagpole. Such one-upmanship borders on the absurd. When the North constructed a two-story building in the Joint Security Area at Panmunjom, the South responded with a three-story building, only to have the North counter-respond by adding another story to their building. During one set of negotiations at Panmunjom, no formal agreement was made to allow for biological breaks. Perceiving the use of restroom facilities to be a sign of weakness, neither side flinched. No bathroom breaks were taken by any of the negotiators during the eleven-hour meeting, thus the encounter was dubbed the "Battle of the Bladders."

While overlooking Kijong-dong, propaganda messages (in Korean) were blasted over loudspeakers praising the brilliance of their leader, Kim Jong-un, and the horrors of Western culture. For entertainment, propaganda operas or patriotic marching tunes are played. Even though an agreement was reached in 2004 to end the twenty-hour-a-day loudspeaker broadcasts, on this day, I heard them blaring. One of the ROK (Republic of Korea) solders informed me the propaganda messages can be heard when tourists are present; but once the tourists leave, the South blasts their own propaganda northward, specifically K-Pop and Gangnam Style.

What brings me to this particular hilltop overlooking Kijong-dong is an attempt to understand how yesterday's history is fabricated to justify today's oppressions. Kijong-dong is a physical human construction to signify a narrative designed to justify current state authorities. It matters little if Kijong-dong is real. Empty physical cities are not the only masks for reality; narratives themselves—stories, or more specifically histories—also serve a purpose as persuasive and effective as Kijong-dong. Care in the construction of history is as crucial and painstaking as the construction of uninhabited villages. History creates, maintains, and sustains powerful social structures responsible for much of the world's hopelessness. Just as a city rises from nothingness to reflect a certain reality, so too is history fabricated to correspond with that same reality.

PART I: The Ideological Construction of History

The question, "What is history but a fable agreed upon?" is accredited to Napoleon Bonaparte. Whether he actually said it or not is unknown, and really unimportant. For the purposes of this first chapter, let's agree on the fable that he did utter these words of wisdom. (Re)membering has little to do with what actually occurred; instead we (dis)member (his)story to serve whatever metanarrative we claim as universal truth. Writing history is a fable, a form of propaganda whose function is to serve the political agenda of those whom society privileges and to justify past atrocities implemented to serve the interests of previous generations. The fable we call history is, like Kijong-dong, a mirage. I write this chapter after standing on the arbitrary line where the Cold War of yesteryear continues to rage. As I gaze north from the DMZ border, I contemplate the history constructed for those on the other side of this line. Specifically, I ponder *Koguryŏ*.

The creation of the "*Koguryŏ* cult" testifies to how ancient history is rewritten to justify the current religious and political "*Juché*[1] ideology" of North Korea. In the seventh century BCE, the Korean Peninsula was divided into three kingdoms: Silla in the southeast, Paekje in

---

1. *Juché* can mean "self-sufficiency," or "self-significance," or "self-importance." Kim Il Sung is credited with developing the Marxist-humanist ideology that supposedly is studied throughout the world. This worldview ideology, according to secondary school textbooks, "is the most scientific and most revolutionary view, for man is placed at the center of everything" (Lankov 2013: 67; Hyok 2004: 52).

the southwest, and Koguryŏ in the north (which stretched into modern northeast China). These kingdoms constantly fought each other until the sixth century, when a recently unified China invaded Koguryŏ in the north as Silla invaded from the south, forcing Koguryŏ to unsuccessfully fight on two fronts. After Silla's victory, it repelled the Chinese and unified, for the first time, the Korean state. This history is analogically problematic for the North because Silla (South Korea) with the help of the superpower of its time, China (like the USA today), vanquished Koguryŏ (North Korea). So, North Korea needs alternative facts. In their history books, Koguryŏ is reimagined as the most advanced kingdom on the peninsula, experiencing a perpetual golden age. Never fully conquered by Silla, Koguryŏ emerged in the tenth century CE, unifying the peninsula for the first time with power resting in the north (Lankov 2007: 43–45).

Supremacy for North Korea's capital, Pyongyang, required the existence of the city prior to the Koguryŏ kingdom. So archaeologists "discovered" Old Chosŏn, the most advanced civilization humanity has ever known (according to North Korean scholars), which existed around present-day Pyongyang (even though most scholars believed Old Chosŏn was located in northeast China on the Liadong Peninsula). When authentic archaeological evidence contradicted this official history, it necessitated the destruction of such artifacts. This occurred when the remains of two-thousand-year-old Chinese commandaries were discovered, indicating that Chinese occupation laid the foundation of present-day Korean culture and statehood. And when Kim Il Sung, in 1993, needed archaeologists to find the tomb of Tangun, the alleged founder of Old Chosŏn and offspring of the she-bear, the tomb was immediately discovered near the nation's capital, thus providing Pyongyang with five thousand years of history (Lankov 2007: 80–81).

Ancient and modern history must be creatively (re)membered. Not only does "might make right," but might also makes truth. North Korea illustrates how the Kim Dynasty is able to impose what is true (history) and what is right upon a majority of their compatriots. Yeonmi Park, who fled North Korea as a thirteen-year-old girl, repeats what many defectors discovered—the history they were taught was false (2015: 22). Many North Korean defectors to the South still believe Kim Il Sung was a great hero. Defensive comments include: "[He] was not a bad person"; "Not a bad human"; "Can't hate him"; "Everyone cried when he died" (Hassig and Oh 2009: 183–84).

Constructed history creates identity, beliefs, meaning, and purpose.

To dispute history, to dispute what everyone says is truth, is not normal; in fact, it is quite abnormal. In his memoirs, Hyok Kang, who went through the North Korean education system, recalled:

> And like all the others—even if today, with hindsight, I may give the impression of mocking [the Kims as demigods]—I can assure you that at the time I swallowed it whole. I was inspired by an unshakeable faith. Although my classmates were unaware of it, I saw reassuring lights glowing from the two Kims; they alone could light our way and improve our gloomy lives. They were fabulous, great-hearted, heroic characters without whom the "people," all of us, were lost, destined to be cast into darkness of death. I was convinced that it was thanks to their endless love of the fatherland that we had managed to survive this far. (2004: 47)

Schoolchildren learn that Great Leader Kim Il Sung single-handedly launched the Korean Communist movement when he founded the Anti-Imperialist Union in 1926 at the age of fourteen (Lankov 2013: 52–53). Although Kim Il Sung did partake in some minor skirmishes against the Japanese colonial powers, he spent most of the 1930–40s period in exile at a Soviet Union military base in Boyazk, far from the ravages of war. His Soviet connection was rewritten in the 1960s when a schism developed between Pyongyang and Moscow, placing him instead at Paektu—Korea's highest and most sacred mountain located on the border with China and the locale of centuries-old shamanist traditions.

Pilgrimages today are still made to witness the glass-encased *kuho*, "slogan trees," where revolutionary sayings were supposedly carved by the camp's guerrilla soldiers. Some of these slogans supposedly dating to the 1940s include references to *Juché*, even though the term is first coined and used by Kim Il Sung in 1955 (Lankov 2013: 39–40; Martin 2004: 48, 109; Park 2015: 22). From Paektu, Kim Il Sung single-handedly led his guerrilla forces to drive out the Japanese invaders (who occupied Korea from 1910 till the end of the Second World War); even though it was the US attacks at Hiroshima and Nagasaki along with invading Russian troops that expelled the Japanese. Nevertheless, North Korean history has Kim Il Sung defeating the Japanese with no participation by the Russians or Americans (Hyok 2004: 152; Jin-Sung 2014: 127).

When Kim Jong Il was tapped to be the political successor, even though he had no political credentials, North Korean history also placed him in Paektu fighting a guerrilla war beside his father, though

11

he would have been three years old by the time World War II ended. Although born in the Soviet Union military base at Khabarovsk, one of the Paektu's *kuho* serves as a marker to Kim Jong Il's birthplace while others show where he studied and played (Lankov 2007: 39–40; Martin 2004: 390). By the time he turned eleven he was helping his father orchestrate the Korean War: "Sometimes he sat up all night together with Comrade Kim Il Sung at the table for mapping out a plan of operation, asking about the situation of the front, thinking of how to frustrate the intention of the enemy and learning Comrade Kim Il Sung's outstanding commanding art" (Hassig and Oh 2009: 55).

Both Kim Il Sung and Kim Jong Il were not only portrayed as supreme humans but credited with magical powers able to transcend time and space. A 2006 *Nodong Sinmun* article titled "Military-First Teleporting" reported that Kim Jong Il was able to appear in one location and then suddenly appear in a different place, "like a flash of lightning." His teleporting abilities were so quick, US satellites orbiting overhead were unable to track his movements (Hassig and Oh 2009: 55). He allegedly wrote 1,500 books during his three years at the university, and was also able to control the weather with his thoughts (Park 2015: 47).

According to the North Korean history textbooks, Japanese atrocities during the occupation of Korea pale in comparison to the Americans who have been trying to enslave Korea since the 1860s. Christian missionaries, according to the textbooks, have a history of participating in sadistically sacrificing Korean children. One textbook story recounts a starving Korean child who stole an apple from the orchard of a foreign missionary. When caught, the missionary etched the word "thief" in acid on the child's forehead (Hyok 2004: 51). Today, Americans brutalize, oppress, and impoverish South Korea who look to the North for their hope and salvation (Lankov 2007: 47). The Korean War supposedly broke out when the US ordered South Koreans to invade the North; but they were repelled and within a few hours, driven back through a masterful counteroffensive directed by the Supreme Leader. The reality is the North invaded the South, causing a US counteroffensive that pushed Northern troops to its border with China only to incite Chinese troops to enter the conflict, pushing US and South Korean troops to the thirty-eighth parallel where today's border between the Koreas is set. According to North Korean history, the war did not end with an armistice, but rather, with an outright victory led by Kim Il Sung over US imperialism (Jin-Sung 2014: 127).

Animosity toward the US can be detected in a typical math quiz that primary students are required to answer: "In a South Korean city occupied by the wolf-like US Army, 2884 school-age children cannot attend school. Of them, 1561 are polishing shoes, while others are begging for food. How many children are begging for food in the Yankee-occupied city?" (Lankov 2007: 47). According to Grace Ji-Sun Kim, who served as my conversation partner in the writing of this chapter, maybe North Korea's animosity toward the US has less to do with ideology and more to do with the decimation of the Korean people during the war. In the course of three years, the US/UN forces flew 1,040,708 sorties in Korea and dropped 386,037 tons of bombs and 32,357 tons of napalm (2007). General Curtis LeMay, responsible for the Korean incineration campaigns, remarked: "After destroying North Korea's 78 cities and thousands of her villages, and killing countless numbers of her civilians, over a period of three years or so we killed off—what—twenty percent of the population" (Rhodes, 1995: 53).[2] This comes to about 8 or 9 million people. So maybe North Korea's animosity has less to do with ideology, and more to do with a US military strategy that genocidally eliminated 20 percent of the population—men, women, and children.

According to Grace Ji-Sun Kim, North Korean acts of belligerence, like firing a missile into the sea, usually occur in April, around the same time the United States conducts military exercises. She believes the US, specifically its military, is probably a major impediment to unification. Nonetheless, South Korea's own historical interpretation is engineered to foster the impression that everything and everyone from North Korea, because they are "red commies," is evil, bad, and the enemy. Grace Ji-Sun Kim recounts a conversation once held with the North Korean ambassador to the United Nations in New York City, where she was hoping to press the government to release Kenneth Bae.[3] She speaks of the sleepless nights leading up to the meeting, brought about by an anxiety rooted in years of indoctrination in which North Koreans were thought to kidnap and kill South Koreans. But as the conversation progressed, the apprehension vanished. North Kore-

2. In a refreshing moment of honesty, Robert McNamara, Secretary of Defense during the Kennedy and Johnson administrations, said in the 2003 Oscar-winning documentary by Errol Morris, *The Fog of War: Eleven Lessons from the Life of Robert S. McNamara*: "[General Curtis] LeMay [primary architect of Japanese firebombing] under whom I served during World War II as an analyst of US bombers' efficiency and effectiveness, said, 'If we'd lost the war, we'd all have been prosecuted as war criminals.' And I think he's right. He, and I'd say I, were behaving as war criminals. LeMay recognized that what he was doing would be thought immoral if his side had lost. But what makes it immoral if you lose and not immoral if you win?"

3. Kenneth Bae is an Evangelical Korean-American missionary sentenced to fifteen years of imprisonment in April 2013 for allegedly planning the overthrow the North Korean government. He was released, along with fellow American Matthew Todd Miller, in November 2014.

ans, she discovered, were like us—not the personification of evil. The people, she argues, should not be identified with a few leaders in the government. Grace Ji-Sun Kim does hope for eventual unification of the Korean peninsula, underscoring the advanced age and mortality of the more hardline older generation.

Historical despots of old relied on iron chains and brutality to constrain compatriots. Today, the more potent instrument of binding and restraint is that of story—the power of constructed ideas, worldviews, and historical interpretation. The chains of ideas prove a stronger link because they are made from what the compatriots believe are their own work, unlike shackles of iron or steel that fall victim to time and corrosion (Foucault 1995: 102–3). Imprisoning compatriots' minds is not limited to totalitarian regimes run by despots; they can be just as effective within democracies.

We Are All North Korea

The construction of history is not limited to North Korea. In a real sense, we are all North Korea. In fact, the Western colonization of the world's minds, specifically those of the subalterns, is more insidious because it coats global oppressive structures with a veneer of utopian high-minded-sounding terms like liberty, human rights, freedom, and democracy. Eurocentric philosophical thought and movements, regardless of how lofty they might sound, remain oppressive to those relegated to colonized spaces. Philosophical enlightenment contributions, such as the French Revolution's battle cry for *Liberté, Egalité, Fraternité* was never meant for her future colonies in Vietnam nor Algiers. Freedom is not for the "inferior" in need of civilization and chistianization. Even the US rhetorical end to our daily pledge of "liberty and justice for all" was never meant to include those from African descent or the country's neighbors south of the border.

Eurocentric philosophical thought was constructed for the colonizers, not her colonies or those among the colonized who followed their stolen raw material and cheap labor to the center of Empires. A progressive history of abstract philosophical thought must be constructed to reconcile the quest for liberty and equality among whites with their purposeful exclusion of those whom they colonized. The issue is not so much hypocrisy on the part of the colonizer spewing rhetoric about liberty, but rather, philosophically justifying oppression through freedom-based language. The move to the abstract serves the crucial purpose of obscuring the economic need of dispossessing and disenfranchising the colonized and their descendants. Universal Eurocentric concepts of rights blinds the oppressed of the concrete feet-on-the-ground reality of oppression at the hands of such freedom-loving whites.

Yet, in spite of the construction of history to justify oppression by white colonizers, it becomes easier to criticize North Korea for its own construction of history devised to perpetuate a hopeful national narrative that justifies current political structures; easy because North Korea is perceived as the enemy, a totalitarian regime; easy because the US has defined them as a member of the "axis of evil."[4] And yet, what is peddled as history in the United States is just as hopeful (a city upon a hill), constructed for the purpose of establishing and undergirding power relationships detrimental to marginalized communities—domestic and foreign. Even if an attempt were made to provide an "objective" reading of the Kim political dynasty or even the US experience, such a venture would be fraught with pitfalls. Because archives are ambiguous, contradictory, and incomplete, history becomes whichever archival evidence the interpreter of history selects to design the narrative of what occurred in the past. History is all too often constructed to justify the superiority of those in power—and those doing the constructing, which in turn is presented as an objective metanarrative.

The construction of a history that perpetuates the personality cult of Kim Jong-un in North Korea is not so different than the construction of a history that perpetuates the hegemonic cult of white supremacy in the United States. In practice, the task of privileging one historical narrative as objective and superior is accomplished by silencing all contradictory voices, as demonstrated by the Tucson Unified School District whose 2011 actions (deemed constitutional in 2013 by a federal judge) forced Arizona school districts to eliminate ethnic studies programs because they were deemed un-American and supposedly taught hatred and ethnic unrest. To facilitate the process, they released the titles of books they had banned to avoid "biased, political and emotionally charged" teaching. Teachers are encouraged to stay away from any works where race, ethnicity, and oppression are central themes.[5]

4. North Korea, along with Iran and Iraq, were described as the "axis of evil" by then-President George W. Bush during his 2002 State of the Union Address, for their supposed involvement in sponsoring terrorism and seeking weapons of mass destruction.
5. Michael Martinez, "Arizona Education Chief Moves to Ban Ethnic Studies in Tucson Schools," CNN, January 5, 2011; Marc Lacey, "Rift in Arizona as Latino Class Is Found Illegal," The New York Times,

Among the books banned are: *Critical Race Theory* by Richard Delgado; Jean Stefancic's *500 Years of Chicano History in Pictures*, edited by Elizabeth Martinez; *Message to Aztlán* by Rodolfo "Corky" Gonzales; *Pedagogy of the Oppressed* by Paulo Freire; and *Rethinking Columbus: The Next 500 Years* by Bill Bigelow.[6] To read these books in a classroom is a violation of Arizona House Bill 2281, which specifically states: "A school district or charter school in this state shall not include in its program of instruction any courses or classes that include any of the following: 1. Promote the overthrow of the United States government; 2. Promote resentment toward a race or class of people; 3. Are designed primarily for pupils of a particular ethnic group; 4. Advocate ethnic solidarity instead of the treatment of pupils as individuals."[7]

Whereas Arizona banned books to silence contradictory historical perspectives, Texas attempted to create history in its own image—specifically a white image (even though more than half of the students in Texas primary and secondary schools are Latinx, most from Mexican descent). For years, the Latinx community petitioned the Texas State Board of Education to be represented in the curricula. In response, a 500-page textbook titled *Mexican American Heritage* ($69.95) made the proposed list of textbooks to be considered for the 2017–18 academic year. In fact, it was the only book on the list dealing with a Latinx perspective. Unfortunately, the history narrated in the textbook concerning Mexican Americans was as problematic as the history presented in North Korea.[8]

The textbook links Mexican Americans to undocumented immigration, which is then conflated with poverty, crime, and the drug trade. The 1960s Chicano/a movement for civil rights is presented as threatening of and in opposition to whites. "Chicanos," according to the book, "adopted a revolutionary narrative that opposed Western civi-

January 7, 2011; and Cindy Carcamo, "Judge Upholds Arizona Law Banning Ethnic Studies," *Los Angeles Times*, March 12, 2013.

6. Roberto Cintli Rodriguez, "Arizona's 'banned' Mexican American Books," *The Guardian*, January 18, 2012.

7. http://www.azleg.gov/legtext/49leg/2r/bills/hb2281s.pdf.

8. It should be noted that the link to the textbook on the publisher's website, Momentum Learning, failed to work when I attempted to read the textbook. Several attempts were made to either obtain a review copy or a working link to segments of the book. After several fruitless conversations with the staff at Momentum Learning, I contacted the publishing house owner, Cynthia Dunbar (and former member of the Texas State Board of Education). An exchange of emails dated June 13, 2016 concluded with a pledge by her to provide me with a copy of the textbook and/or a link to the book. As of the date of this book's publication, I am still waiting to examine the textbook for myself. Unable to obtain access, my critique of the textbook is based on those who were able to obtain access prior to it becoming unavailable. Those who reviewed the textbook cited over 140 factual errors.

lization and wanted to destroy this society." Social division and polarization are attributed to Mexican pride. "College youth attempted to force their campuses to provide indigenismo-oriented curriculum, Spanish-speaking faculty and scholarships for poor and illegal students." "During the Cold War," the textbook continues, "as the United States fought Communism worldwide, these kinds of separatist and supremacy doctrines were concerning. While solidarity with one's heritage was understood, Mexican pride at the expense of American culture did not seem productive." As per the textbook, "Chicano philosophy, which pervades urban Latino areas, often reinforces the idea that rebellion against the establishment is part of the true Mexican identity. High school and college youth may refuse to attend class, speak English or learn certain subjects because they perceive injustice in the school system, sometimes led by well-meaning Latino adults. This hinders prosperity because adequate employment depends on many years of intense study."[9]

The textbook goes on to editorialize: "Pressure exists that those of Mexican origin are not 'Mexican enough' or do not have enough sympathy and respect for their roots if they venture beyond the Spanish-speaking world." "The belief," the textbook continues, "along with the idea that Latin culture must be held up as superior and separate from American culture, holds many back today." Making Cubans the model Hispanics, the book argues that "Cubans seemed to fit into Miami well, for example, and find their niche in the business community; Mexicans, on the other hand, seemed more ambivalent about assimilating into the American system and accepting American values. . . . The concern many Mexican-Americans feel disconnected from American cultures and values is still present."[10]

---

9. Yanan Wang, "Proposed Texas Textbook Says Some Mexican Americans 'Wanted to Destroy' U.S. Society," *The Washington Post*, May 24, 2016; and Raul A. Reyes, "Texas Mexican Heritage Textbook a Racist Travesty," CNN, May 25, 2016; Cindy Cassares, "A Textbook on Mexican Americans That Gets Their History Wrong? Oh, Texas," *The Guardian*, May 31, 2016.

10. Yanan Wang, "Proposed Texas Textbook Says Some Mexican Americans 'Wanted to Destroy' U.S. Society," *The Washington Post*, May 24, 2016; and Raul A. Reyes, "Texas Mexican Heritage Textbook a Racist Travesty," CNN, May 25, 2016. Besides the negative portrayals of Mexican Americans, many of the "facts" in the textbook are simply wrong. For example, it refers to the tango, rumba, and salsa as Mexican dances, when in actuality they are Argentine, Cuban, and Puerto Rican respectively. It celebrates writers who are neither Mexican American nor Mexican, like Isabel Allende (Chilean), Gabriel Garcia Marquez (Colombian), or Paulo Coelho (Brazilian). More importantly, the Anglo land grabs from Mexicans holding land title during the late nineteenth century are portrayed as an exaggeration, claiming "the majority was legally sold." See Raul A. Reyes, "Texas Mexican Heritage Textbook a Racist Travesty," CNN, May 25, 2016; and Cindy Cassares, "A Textbook on Mexican Americans That Gets Their History Wrong? Oh, Texas," *The Guardian*, May 31, 2016.

In September 2016, the Texas State Board of Education held a hearing where protestors voiced their opposition to the adaptation of the controversial textbook. About 200 academics, lawmakers and scholars rallied to urge the Board to reject the offensive "official" history textbook.[11] A week after the September meeting, according to email exchanges among Board members obtained through a Public Information Act request, Board member David Bradley (R-Beaumont), who referred to textbook protestors as "left-leaning, radical Hispanic activists,"[12] wrote to fellow Board member Thomas Ratliff (R-Mount Pleasant) indicating he would prefer to prevent giving critics of the book the pleasure of witnessing the text voted down. He suggested board members leave and skip the November vote altogether: "A lack of a quorum on [sic] would be nice. Deny the Hispanics a record vote. The book still fails."[13] A second hearing was scheduled for November 16, 2016, where, due to organized protest, the Texas State Board of Education was forced finally to reject the textbook.[14] Irrespective of the final decision, the textbook served its purpose in signifying how the dominant culture writes (whites) history regardless of facts, and when held accountable, refuses to admit their subjectivity.

The book's authors, Jaime Riddle and Valarie Angle, are neither Latinx, nor historians, nor sociologists; neither is recognized as an academic expert within Mexican American, Chicano, or Latinx studies—or any other academic discipline for that matter. The company Momentum Learning, the textbook's publisher, is owned by Cynthia Dunbar, a former member of the Texas State Board of Education (2007–2011). Dunbar, in her own book, *One Nation Under God: How the Left Is Trying to Erase What Made Us Great*, refers to the public education system as "tyrannical."[15] More recently, she compared the LGBT civil rights movement to Nazism.[16] Another School Board member, Mary Lou Bruner, elected in 2016, claimed President Obama "has a soft spot for homosexuals because of the years he spent as a male prostitute in his

11. Mary Tuma, "Teaching Truthiness: Activists, Lawmakers Call on State Board of Education to Reject Racist Mexican-American Textbook," *The Austin Chronicle*, September 16, 2016.
12. Patrick Michels, "Mexican-American Studies Summit Takes on 'Racist' Textbook," *The Observer*, June 16, 2016.
13. Mary Tuma, "SBOE Member Wants to 'Deny Hispanics' Vote on Racist Mexican-American Textbook," *The Austin Chronicle*, September 21, 2016.
14. Brian Latimer, "Texas Rejects Mexican-American Studies Textbook Seen as Racist," NBC News, November 16, 2016.
15. Yanan Wang, "Proposed Texas Textbook Says Some Mexican Americans 'Wanted to Destroy' U.S. Society," *The Washington Post*, May 24, 2016.
16. Jeremy W. Peters, "Donald Trump Keeps Distance in G.O.P. Platform Fight on Gay Rights," *The New York Times*, July 10, 2016.

twenties. That is how he paid for his drugs."[17] The School Board does appoint a panel of 140 reviewers to check for textbook accuracy; however, only three on the panel are actual historians—most have no academic standing.[18]

This is not the first attempt by the Texas School Board to construct reality. They have fought against textbooks that include evolution and global warming (the latter deemed a hoax); at the same time, they have advocated for school material that links Islamic history with terrorism and insists that Moses and the Ten Commandments were foundational to the US Founding Fathers.[19] The current Texas social studies textbooks downplay slavery and fail to mention Jim and Jane Crow laws or the Ku Klux Klan, insisting that the causes of the Civil War were, in order, sectionalism, states' rights, and then slavery. Slavery was a side issue, according to School Board member Pat Hardy. And during segregation, African Americans and whites had "similar buildings, buses, and teachers. . . . Sometimes, however, the buildings, buses, and teachers for all-black schools were lower in quality."[20] Elsewhere, Joseph McCarthy's blacklisting of Americans is justified because communists did indeed infiltrate the government during the Cold War.[21] The high school history book claims "the minimum wage remains one of the New Deal's most controversial legacies"; it also portrays the United Nations as undermining US sovereignty.[22] In a recent Texas textbook, *World Geography* published by McGraw-Hill, slaves were referred to as "workers from Africa."[23] Of course, it would be easy to simply dismiss the Texan construction of history (and science) as an aberration; however, because of Texas's dominance of the school textbook market, purchasing nearly fifty million books yearly, decisions made in Texas disproportionately affect other states as they purchase books written to meet Texas's standards due to bulk purchasing savings.

Regardless if the history of the marginalized is suppressed (as per

17. Yanan Wang, "A Texan Who Called Obama a Gay Prostitute May Soon Control What Goes in Children's Textbooks," *The Washington Post*, March 4, 2016.
18. Zack Kopplin, "Was Moses a Founding Father?" *The Atlantic*, November 25, 2014.
19. Terrence Stutz, "Texas Education Board Approves Science Book That Fully Covers Evolution," *The Dallas Morning News*, November 22, 2013; idem, "Texas Board of Education Delays Action on Textbooks Amid Revisions," *Dallas Morning News*, November 18, 2014.
20. Emma Brown, "Texas Officials: Schools Should Teach That Slavery Was 'Side Issue' to Civil War," *The Washington Post*, July 5, 2015; Zachary Roth, "Texas Textbooks Complain about Taxes, Downplay Segregation," MSNBC, September 11, 2014.
21. Zack Kopplin, "Was Moses a Founding Father?" *The Atlantic*, November 25, 2014.
22. "Rewriting History? Texas Tackles Textbook Debate," CBS/AP, September 16, 2014.
23. Zoë Schlanger, "Company Apologizes for Texas Textbook Calling Slaves 'Workers': 'We Made a Mistake,'" *Newsweek*, October 5, 2015.

the Tucson model) or rewritten (as per the Texas model), a national amnesia leads to, and justifies, an attitude of exceptionalism that exempts the ruling class from following the moral principles imposed upon those subjugated. Teaching amnesia benefits the neoconservative acceptance of the United States' unique role as "a beacon for democracy" and a force for global neoliberal free trade. US foreign policy and military intervention are acceptable because of our good and noble intentions, even though these same foreign policies and military interventions would be condemned if implemented by other sovereign nations. Exceptionalism, due to a fabricated view of ourselves as a force for good in the world (as opposed to the "Evil Empire," or the "Axis of Evil"), facilitates the suspension of moral and ethical imperatives imposed on others as a means of checking power. Recall General LeMay's firebombing of North Korea, and previously of Japan.

Thinking one uniquely represents the good develops a hubris that obstructs meaningful dialogue to foster a more just and liberative world. American exceptionalism is but the latest jingoistic, white-supremacist moral initiative based on a constructed history of pre-eminence. Previous generations of Euroamericans considered it their birthright, due to their skin pigmentation, to enforce those whom they considered inferior to labor and sacrifice for the benefit of all whites. Jim and Jane Crow, and slavery before it, ensured that benefits and privileges would not reside in the hands of nonwhites. Today, exceptionalism ensures that benefits and privileges continue to reside in the hands of "real" Americans, understood to be white Americans. This explains why the majority of the world's resources flow in our direction to support about 6 percent of the world's population. Politicians who insist they will "make America great again" justify their campaign promise through a historical construct exempting the United States from the global ethical rule of order required from civilized nations.

PART II: The Inherently Exclusionary Nature of "Universal" Histories

If histories are constructs benefiting the privileged, why do we accept them as truth? My intentions are not to dismiss or refute the existence of universal truth, but rather to be highly suspicious of such claims. No doubt there are those who would insist on some universal truth we can comprehend either through revelation or reason; nevertheless, whatever truth might be, if it even exists, remains beyond our capacities to determine with any certainty. The cacophonous claims of religions, ideologies, and philosophies are all rooted in particular constructed histories claiming to be the truth; yet, they are all equal in their inability to validate with certitude. Unfortunately, the limited physical and temporal space to which we are all confined prevents us from occupying any external position of certainty. Universalities cannot be confirmed by human beings, as they are unable to observe reality beyond the society and time span to which they are bound.

How then do we conduct rigorous analysis without resorting to simplistic answers provided by universalities? Setting aside utopias and metanarratives, our quest ceases to be for some elusive universal truth, as we instead focus on the constructed truth or history we are asked to believe. Such a quest is more crucial because constructed truth establishes and reveals power relationships. "The real political task in a society such as ours," Michel Foucault claims, "is to criticize the working of institutions which appear to be both neutral and independent; to criticize them in such a manner that the political violence which has always exercised itself obscurely through them will be unmasked, so that one can fight them" (1974: 171).

Thinkers like Foucault have convinced me, in the absence of knowing any universalities, that we are left with a small minority deciding for the rest of us what is truth.[24] As a Christian ethicist I confess my interest and bias lies in pursuing a liberationist way to live (orthopraxis), rather than the search for some theological truth (orthodoxy). A critical liberative ethical analysis can reveal how power operates to legitimize and normalize oppressive structures. Such an analysis can be facilitated through a critical adaptation of Foucauldian thought, assisting us to move beyond a Christian rhetoric (such as hope) that contributes to oppressive social structures.

Take two examples of the humane treatment of the insane offered by Samuel Tuke[25] and Philippe Pinel,[26] as illustrated by Foucault in his first major work, *Madness and Civilization*. Both Tuke and Pinel have historically been presented as enlightened clinician reformers to the bru-

---

24. I am keenly aware of the absence of the poor, the marginalized, women, and the colonized in Foucault's writings. Even Foucault's work is constructed with certain exclusions. Nevertheless, we begin with Foucault, in spite of his limitations, to help us better grasp how power operates.

25. Samuel Tuke, a Quaker, is considered a mental health so-called reformer, who institutionalized moral therapy in England during the eighteenth century.

26. Philippe Pinel, a French physician, developed a moral therapy during the eighteenth century. He is considered by some as the father of modern psychiatry. Pinel's "enlightened" system of moral therapy was tied to the new middle class established after the French Revolution where madness belonged to social failure.

tal and ignorant treatment of the insane during previous ages. Foucault instead argues that the so-called neutral scientific approach to medical treatment of the insane, as introduced by Tuke and Pinel, are, in reality, masking an attempt to domesticate abbreviations to conventional bourgeois moral sensibilities. Normalizing and legitimizing insanity as mental illness (as opposed to, say, demonic possession per premodern thinking) was a constructed concept with questionable moral, ethical, and social commitments.

Tuke's insane asylum, known as the York Retreat, was like a family where inmates, as children, learned to honor and respect the authority of the father—who happened to be Tuke himself. Chains were removed as the inmates learned religion and morality and participated in work. The chains, however, could always be placed back on the inmate if the inmate disobeyed. Because the insane were constantly watched for hints of madness, they learned to watch themselves. In the asylum Pinel managed, this middle-class norm was the ethical standard, just as it was for the society as a whole. Insanity was defined as rejection of this middle-class moral standard, a nonconformity prevalent among lower-class populations. The asylum became a religious domain minus the religion, "a domain of pure morality, of ethical uniformity." Moral uniformity is linked to social denunciation where punishment for nonconformity was swift, severe, and repetitive until the patient learned not only to internalize the proper behavior expected, but be thankful for the punishment meted out as a necessary means toward a "cure" (1961: 257–59, 267–68).

Disciplinary control (power), as illustrated by the so-called neutral implementation of Tuke's and Pinel's modern medical treatment of the clinically insane, is maintained, according to Foucault, through the techniques of 1) hierarchical observation (the gaze), 2) the normalization of judgment, and 3) the examination. People can thus be controlled through the mere act of gazing. The power to observe corrects deviant behavior by coercing the one defined by society as abnormal to become how society defines normal. The mere possibility of being watched forces the object of the gaze to internalize the power relation. The examination of the clinic's patients to measure the process of curing insanity combines the gaze with normalizing judgment through "the deployment of force and the establishment of truth" (1975: 184). Force, or power, is interconnected with the establishment of truth—for our purposes, the "truth" of history. To exert power is to construct the "truth" of history, and to know the "truth" of history is to exert power.

What then is the truth of history? The question is highly problematic because it assumes there exists one truth and one history. If we begin by recognizing that if truth does exist we finite humans are incapable of knowing it, then whatever we claim to be truth is whatever those with power claim truth to be. Power is what produces truth. "There is no power relation," Foucault reminds us, "without the correlative constitution of a field of knowledge, nor any knowledge that does not presuppose and constitute at the same time power relations." Thus, the writing of history is not due to an interest in past events; rather, it constitutes writing the history of the present (1975: 27, 31). Historian and conversation partner Albert Hernández reminds me of Fernand Braudel's dictum: "The past is about the present." The past does not exist in some forgotten archive waiting to be discovered. Whatever we can know about the past is inspired by and understood through the prism of the present.

Writing the history of the present occurs within the intersection of power and knowledge. So often history is controlled by individuals with the power to gaze, normalize, legitimize, and impose their version of truth upon the majority. Each new present requires the construction of a new past. Once truth is constructed, to question said truth is to question reality—a symptom of insanity—and as such, requires—as a humane response—institutionalization. Those who dared to see with their own eyes have been dismissed as insane and locked away in mental institutions, as was the case in the Soviet Union and China.[27]

If not construed as mad, those who refuse to accept reality are seen as a perversion endangering the rest of society, and to safeguard the well-being of the whole, these individuals—like a cancer—must be cut out. If not disappeared, they must at least be humiliated or permanently silenced, as was the case with many US-backed military dictatorships in Latin America during the 1960s through the 80s. Proper social behavior and thought are codified through the creation of a false history, especially a salvation history, which demands observance and obedience, and which legitimates punishment and ostracization of any deviation. But in order to know when deviation is afoot, surveillance is required by the ruling paternal figure, whether it be Kim Il Sung or Kim

27. During the early 1970s, reports began to reach the West about the incarceration of political and religious dissidents, who were locked away in maximum-security psychiatric asylums without any medical justification. For Soviet rulers, to repudiate the legitimized State was itself a symptom of an unwell mind. Similar tactics have been employed in China, from the 1949 Revolution to the more recent treatment of Falun Gong adherents, in which critics of the state have been deemed by authorities to be mentally unstable (Bonnie 2002: 137, 141).

Jong Il, Tuke or Pinel. "Over all these endeavors on the part of clinical thought to define its methods and scientific norms," Foucault reminds us,

> hovers the great myth of a pure Gaze that would be pure Language; a speaking eye. It would scan the entire . . . field, taking in and gathering together each of the singular events that occurred within it; and as it saw, as it saw even more and more clearly, it would be turned into speech that states and teaches; the truth, which events, in their repetitions and convergence, would outline under its gaze, would, by this same gaze and in the same order, be reserved, in the form of teaching, to those who do not know and have not yet seen. This peeking eye would be the servant of things and the master of truth. (1963: 140–41)

Constructing History to Construct Hope and Superiority

The quest for some general unifying theory explaining the movement of history is highly problematic. To be anti-Hegelian is to question progress as time marches forward, and to reject salvation history is to question the theology of hope interwoven into the very fabric of history.[28] The nature of the hope we reject can be seen in the influential work of Jürgen Moltmann: "[I]n the medium of hope our theological concepts become not judgments which nail down reality to what it is, but anticipations which show reality its prospects and its future possibilities. Theological concepts do not give a fixed form to reality, but they are expanded by hope and anticipate future being. . . . [T]hey illuminate reality by displaying its future" (1967: 35–36). Moltmann, like the Christian determinists, attempts to convince us that an eschatological hope rooted in salvation history is the only way by which to interpret reality. While arguing against utopias (1967: 23), he nonetheless creates his own; for once his subjective reality is defined as objective truth, universal Christian faith and action can be understood and implemented. But accepting a historical metanarrative with a purposeful end frustrates our ability to establish an ethical response rooted in our estrangement brought about by the hopeless situation in which the world's disenfranchised find themselves. Eschatology may belong to the frozen chosen, but for humans of flesh and bone residing on the underside, the now belongs to them. To reside in the hopelessness

---

28. Care should be taken not to confuse a dialectical history based on teleological progress as time moves linearly, with a salvation history rooted in the triumphal apocalyptic end of history ushering in the kingdom of God, thus signifying redemption for believers.

of the now is to be cognizant of the joy and disappointment of the moment.

The theology of hope espoused by Moltmann is predicated on the modernist quest for universal meaning to history—which is to say, a fundamentally European way of construing and relating to reality. In other words, modernity as ethos (moral character) is a choice made voluntarily by white Europeans to mark a relation of belonging while determining how this group will think, feel, act, and behave toward the Other (Foucault 1984: 39).

As a product of the so-called Age of Enlightenment modernity is, and always will be, a Eurocentric phenomenon. This is a phenomenon that excludes the periphery where the world's hopeless are situated, and forces critical thought to be directed to the center. G. W. F. Hegel, a metaphysical philosopher, attempted to elucidate the direction and meaning of history by providing a God's-eye view. For Hegel, the philosophy of history interprets a complete and full understanding of the structures, processes, and events associated with the passage of time, through which the meaning and structure of the totality of history can be revealed. "History," for Hegel, as "the process whereby the Spirit discovers itself and its own concept" (1857: 62), is an intelligible movement of time toward the teleological realization of human freedom. It is human freedom achieved through the movement of Spirit in history that constitutes the true meaning of history itself as a process, which is, for Hegel, also fundamentally political (1824: 332–33). Hence Hegel constructs world history as a narrative of political evolution, from the polis, through the Roman Republic and Protestant Revolution toward the freedom of the modern state.

The architectonic of Hegel's narrative of world history is undergirded by a religious philosophical metaphysic that hybridizes Stoicism and German Pietism with Aristoteleanism. At root is the mind of the divine being as immanent in matter. The ultimate reality of God, recognized as Spirit, becomes the axis upon which History and the World turn (1824: 319), which can be grasped and known through the process of pure thought (a return to a pre-Kantian religious-based philosophy).[29] "It must be observed at the outset," Hegel writes, "that the phenomenon we investigate—Universal History—belongs to the realm of *Spirit*. The term 'World' includes both physical and psychical Nature. Physical nature also plays its part in the World's History. . . . But Spirit,

---

29. The reader will notice I maintain a traditional metaphysical interpretation of Hegel's writings.

and the course of its development, is our substantial object. . . . We have in our universal consciousness two realms, the realm of Nature and the realm of Spirit. . . . One may have all sorts of ideas about the Kingdom of God; but it is always a realm of Spirit to be realized and brought about in man" (1824: 16). Philosophy and theology, he writes, "have the Divine as their common object; and although the theology of the Church was a stereotyped dogma, the impulse now arose to justify this body of doctrine in the view of Thought" (1824: 397). Religion and philosophy have the same goal—understanding God.[30]

Of course, and quite important for us here, if understanding God is the goal—and this is achieved in the study of universal history—the goal and the process are both inherently racialized. Hegel's understanding of history maintains that the progressive arc of world history is a movement from East to West. A divine order is imposed upon the direction of human history as the unfolding of human freedom. Northern Europe, specifically the German Spirit, for Hegel, is the Spirit of the new World whose aim becomes the realization of absolute Truth as the unlimited self-determination of Freedom (1824: 341). For Hegel, history is a necessary movement originating in Asia and moving toward Europe, where it arrives at its end as the product of Western civilization and the fullest understanding of God. Europe, for Hegel, is the axial end of History, and the heart of Europe—Germanic-Anglo-Saxon—is the center and end of universal history (1824: 103). His entire enterprise of elucidation of universal and transcendent truth rests on the presupposition of the superiority of Europeans and the inferiority of non-Europeans. We may wonder, here, if Hegel's dismissal of those on the Germanic margins contributes to the philosophical roots of the US exceptionalism previously discussed.

Moreover, it is in Hegel's historiographical methods and practices that we see how his analysis is problematic, most notably his stereotyping of other cultures (specifically Asian, African, Latin American). In his philosophy of history, Hegel presents us with a dialectical movement of Spirit in time through *certain* communities—but not all. Simultaneously, this dialectical movement of Spirit and time is linked by Hegel

---

30. In my conversation with historian Hernandez, he reminds me how for Hegel, the movement of the Spirit is influenced by the human will. If humans were to surrender their hearts and minds to Christ, then individualism would be at the service of God and/or a higher principle. Hernandez wonders if Hegel's philosophy was influenced by Abbot Joachim of Fiore, specifically the abbot's understanding of the third and last stage of salvation history. This third stage began with the pouring of the Spirit on Pentecost, which still moves the Church and the human race toward a redemptive utopian hope.

with the notion of progress, constituted by the evolution of human societies from primitive to advanced states. Progress is measurable by academic, theoretical, technological, and spiritual human advancements. So, in Hegel's genealogical narrative of history, we move from the medieval "dark ages" to the so-called age of Enlightenment, from the superstitious to the rational, from the premodern to the modern. A triumphalist dialectic of the rise and development of Western civilization, or more specifically, Germanic civilization, is fused and conflated with a theological understanding of the self-revelation and manifestation of the mind—or being—of God itself.

In history's march toward the European center, Hegel surgically removes the Iberian Peninsula from the European continent (due to its Africanization through seven hundred years of Moorish Islamic rule). Hegel specifically states that Southern Europe (which includes Spain) is not the bearer of the Spirit, only Germanic-Anglo-Saxons. Likewise, Africa and Latin America are removed from the movement of World History and situated, like Asia, in a state where their "inferiority" is manifest and a negative symbol of history's evolution away from them (1824: 81–82, 96). As if to reinforce this hierarchy as essential and inherent to progress itself, Hegel demarcates the start of modernity as the time when Europeans began to consolidate power over Other people and continents (1824: 99).

We are left to wonder how the undergirding assumptions and assertions of Hegel's macro-history truly resonate among those perceived as too inferior to be included within the progressive movement of Spirit in World History. Do Hegel's explicit biases toward non-Northern Europeans make his entire historical construction so subjective and value-laden as to be of little use to those he dismisses as inferior? Is his constructed account of history void of any possible objective reality independent of his prejudices? Hegel focuses on the interpretation of large metahistorical features instead of the individual praxes and worldviews of those he situates at the margins. Thus, he becomes a creator of mythical historical narratives that deliver ideological meanings of past events not much different, albeit more sophisticated, than the interpreters of North Korea under the Kim dynasty or the Texas school board in the US. Liberationist philosopher Enrique Dussel reminds us that power, domination, and the center are identical (1990: 6). This is all too evident in Hegel's declaration: "In contrast with this absolute right which [Europe] possesses as bearer of the present stage of the world spirit's development, the spirits of other nations are *without rights,* and they, like those whose epoch has passed, *no longer count in world history*" (1820 § 347). The consequences of Hegel's thought relegate the hopeless of the world to a space where they are incapable of contributing to human progress or having an ongoing role in the meaning of history itself. What, then, is the purpose of this space they are called to occupy in World History? To obtain salvation from the missionary generosity of the center by whom they are called to serve.

Resistance Is Futile

The gaze of history normalizes and legitimizes the official narrative, while reinforcing the oppression of those excluded from the story. Disciplinary control or power is exerted and maintained through the techniques of hierarchical observation, the normalization of judgment, and the implementation of an examination. The mere act of gazing corrects deviant behavior, leading the one being observed to self-discipline. In this is the transferal of the techniques of the correction of madness to the correction of political dissent. Foucault's Panopticon is an example of this form of disciplinary technology. In his book *Discipline and Punishment,* Foucault discusses how those who violated the laws of society, or more specifically, the laws of the royal sovereign, were subjected to torture as a form of punishment, in which the goal was revenge for rebelling against the divine authority of the king or queen. Reform meant that the goal of punishment ceased to be revenge and instead became the correction of deviant or abnormal behavior so that the one to be disciplined could be aligned with the norms of society.

In his book, Foucault introduces us to the Panopticon, which he describes as Jeremy Bentham's model prison. The Panopticon was a penal institution designed with a shaded guard tower in the center of the complex, from which the guard could gaze at each prisoner in their individual backlit cells, while the prisoners were unable, because the tower is dark, to gaze back at the guard. "The perfect disciplinary apparatus," Foucault reminds us, "would make it possible for a single gaze to see everything constantly. A central point would be both the source of light illuminating everything, and a locus of convergence for everything that must be known: a perfect eye that nothing would escape and a centre towards which all gazes would be turned" (1975: 173). The gaze of the guard confers power on the observer while denying it to those being observed: the object of information is seen, but does not see—never becoming a subject of communication (1975: 200). The mere possibility of being watched forces the Object of the gaze to internalize the power relation. "He who is subjected to a field of visibility, and who knows it, assumes responsibility for the constraint of power." Think of how you police yourself and do not speed up when the light turns yellow knowing a surveillance camera might be present. Why do you not speed up? Foucault tells us about the one under surveillance:

> [H]e makes them play spontaneously upon himself; he inscribes in himself the power relation in which he simultaneously plays both roles; he becomes the principle of his own subjection. By this very fact, the external power may throw off its physical weight; it tends to the non-corporeal; and, the more it approaches this limit, the more constant, profound and permanent are its effects: it is perpetual victory that avoids any physical confrontation and which is always decided in advance. (1995: 202–3)

The principles gleaned from the panopticon are, of course, not limited to prisons but applicable to any social structure, be it a church, or a classroom, or a neighborhood. Prisoners internalize the norms constructed by prison officials, or church ministers, or schoolteachers, learning to monitor their behavior under the hierarchical gaze so as to conform to what has been deemed normal. For Foucault, it would be naïve to view power as exclusively centralized in the hands of the elite, for power is everywhere, forming and passing through a multitude of institutions. Power becomes most effective, according to Foucault, when it is exercised through coercion that appears entirely natural and neutral. The prison, the insane asylum, the hospital, the grade school, the work center, or any other regulated institution forges a disciplinary power where "a docile body . . . may be subjected, used, transformed and improved" (1975: 136). These institutional locales become religious domains minus religion, domains organized around the pure morality of ethical uniformity.

Docilization of the body, for the ultimate salvation of the body, is accomplished by controlling the space where the body is found (as in the case of the prison); through repetition of drills (as in the case of schoolhouses); or through the standardization of actions deemed normal (as in the case of insane asylums). Docilization moves from physical force to standard bureaucratic procedures. Justice is relieved of its responsibility through an administrative concealment of the penalty itself, thus institutionalizing the violence of the punishment to create ethical uniformity manifested by institutional and societal equilibrium. Rather than instigating punishment to reestablish ethical uniformity,

29

punishment simply reactivates power. This punishment, meted out to an inmate (or patient, or student) for an infraction, is symbolically directed at all potential violators of the norm, all the potentially guilty.

Punishment serves a whole new morality by preventing others from straying from the norm. The fear of punishment ceases to be needed to maintain discipline as all inmates internalize their own discipline. No longer does punishment need to strike the body, for now it strikes the "heart, the thoughts, the will, the inclinations"; in short—the soul. A shift in the "technology of power" has made punishment, which has been effectively used in the past, less effective than the guard's ubiquitous gaze internalized by the inmates. As the eyes of the inmates witnessed and committed to memory the terror of swift punishment, a system of diminishing penalties took effect (1975: 10, 16, 49, 108). The guard in the tower, the power demanding obedience, is disguised as daily normal and legitimate practices, thus moving from control of bodies through punishment to control of souls (now the locus of false consciousness) through the unblinking gaze. The subjectivity of those whom structures privilege becomes the objective norm. No longer are scars caused by some centralized elite.

Power, Foucault argues, is exercised, not possessed. It is not the privilege of the dominant class, but rather the overall effect of their strategic positions. The power to inflict scars on the docile body resides in a multitude of networks (asylums, prisons, countries) interwoven with the political economy of the elite (1975: 26). Because power cannot be limited to the realm of those whom power benefits, replacing the privileged would not suffice in eliminating these networks ingrained in every fiber of what has been constructed as history. The autonomy of a disciplinary structure designed to punish any abnormality will also punish those for whom the structures are designed to privilege in the event they too become "abnormal" and question the prevailing worldview. To gaze upon oneself through the eyes of the dominant culture is the ultimate goal in the colonization of the mind of the oppressed. To gaze upon history is to normalize sociopolitical structures rigged against the flourishing of justice. A similar gaze is also cast toward sacred texts to construct interpretations that control bodies with piety codes rather than liberate bodies from oppression. But these oppressive conditions are not limited to the disenfranchised, for said structures create inhuman existence for both the marginalized and the dominant culture. The dispossessed are denied their humanity by institutionalized violence while those benefiting from said violence lose their humanity in the process.

Trekkies recall the Borg, an alien race that served as a frequent antagonist in the Star Trek franchise. The Borg was a cybernetic species functioning as one mind referred to as "the Collective." The Borg terrified other species, which it "assimilated" into the "collective." The assimilated species lost all that once defined their identity, their culture, their worldview, their abnormalities. When species attempted to fight the Borg, the collective's response was always the same: "Resistance is futile." As part of the Borg, the new species became "normal"—normal as defined by the Borg. Although we need not fear science fiction fantasies of some alien Borg race, nevertheless, the act of assimilation, the instrumental recoding of the body, remains just as terrifying for those hanging on to what defines their uniqueness. For assimilation to succeed, the prisoner, patient, or patriot being gazed upon by those with power to see must adopt and believe a new history, a history constructed to justify and glorify the assimilation process. Philosophizing, theorizing, and theologizing create ideologies in which the creators of thought and history enforce a self-serving reality that reifies the worldview of those whom history privileges and justifies the demand for obeisance and conformity.

Take, for example, Pope Benedict XVI's argument: "Redemption is offered to us in the sense that we have been given hope, trustworthy hope, by virtue of which we can face our present: the present, even if it is arduous, can be lived and accepted if it leads towards a goal, if we can be sure of this goal, and if this goal is great enough to justify the effort of the journey (2007: par. 1). Speaking from the palatial Vatican, it becomes disingenuous to claim an arduous life. Even more, the ideology of some salvation history makes resistance futile, forcing the dissenter to question their own sanity. Easier to assimilate is believing in some heavenly goal that makes the present arduous life acceptable, to commit to actions derived from the dominant worldview, even when said acts are detrimental to our being because of the blessed assurance that our faithfulness in the here-and-now is redeemed in some future eschaton.

However, rather than accepting dominant narratives on the basis of fabled future utopias, praxis that is based on the lived experience and worldviews of the poor and dispossessed is a primary act of resistance. Why? Because it refuses the normalized worldview of those who benefit from the construction of dominant narratives and codes. Resistance may not lead to some liberated utopia; nevertheless, it does enable the liberating process of decolonizing one's mind. In short, it leads to salvation in the here-and-now. That is, of course, a double-edged statement: it is to deny a promised transcendent future, and it is to resist, or reject, any Christian belief or teaching that presumes that to imitate Jesus is to accept abuse, pain, humiliation, and violation as "carrying their cross."[31]

The End of History

Liberation requires a rejection of the official history of the dominant culture. Hegelian historical dialectic is believed by the dominant Eurocentric culture because it affirms those who occupy the center of history. Still, we must ask: Whose history are we reading? Who benefits from the official history? Whose interests does history serve? Who gets to write the history? These questions are asked not to discover, or give voice to a politically correct history; rather, they are to raise the issue of ownership: Who owns history? Because Europeans are, according to Hegel, *the* bearers of the development of the world's Spirit, those relegated to the underside of Eurocentric history are silenced, if not tossed asunder.

The true danger facing marginalized people whose spirit is denied any right is to accept the Hegelian, or any other Eurocentric construct of history as truth. Such truth inherently projects shame onto who they are as a people and demands they relinquish their identity in order to assimilate. For many of the world's wretched, their minds are so colonized they know the history of their oppressors better than their own. To be written out of the story becomes a terrorist act, in which the memory of the marginalized is replaced with the fictitious story of their oppressors, robbing them of identity, of centered-ness, of authentic being. Such a terrorist act is more insidious than physical harm, for it devastates the soul, the spirit, the mind, the very essence of a people. History, after all, is the story of those evolved to a fully realized and achieved humanity. The not-yet human, pivotally rendered in Hegel's master-slave dialectic, have no history. Their current (if any) presence in the story is relegated to when they are encountered by the

---

31. An example of this way of thinking can be found in the Methodist church primer approved by the Methodist General Conference and used throughout the antebellum South. Known as Capers's Catechism, slaves were taught their servitude to whites was God's will and calling for their lives (Hoyt 1991: 27–28). Suffering in the here-and-now will be offset by God's promise of an eschatological glory.

colonizer. Even if those outside of history insist on inclusion, their history, according to Linda Tuhiwai Smith, "is erased before [their] eyes, dismissed as irrelevant, ignored or rendered as the lunatic ravings of drunken old people" (2012: 31). Recall the Mexican American Texas textbook.

The victors of history inscribe their genealogies upon this human metanarrative, emphasizing military victories and political achievements. Such constructed histories become the official history, mirroring the actions and values embodied within the hyper-militaristic dominant culture. Yet, the truth of the Subject is not found in the subject's history. Psychoanalyst Jacques Lacan would have us look for truth in the "locus" of the Other (1977: 286). Precisely for this reason, dominant power must constantly obliterate the Other's "locus" and the Other's history. Left behind from history, specifically salvation history, are all who refuse to believe in the very particular doctrine of the eschaton. But resistance may not necessarily be futile. To seek the voice of those who do not inhabit history—to recall and reclaim forgotten history—is a powerful critique of those with power and privilege.

Those of us who read history in Spanish understand the term as *historia*. In Spanish, *historia* can be translated as "history," but also as "tale, story." *La historia* (history) is a *historia* (story) that recognizes all *historias* (histories/stories) as works of fiction. Even when *historia* is based on true events, all too often it is retold from a romanticized, braggadocio, self-serving (re)membering. All *historias* (histories) are revisionist. Objective historical accounts fail to exist. The question before us is whose revisionist *historia* will become the norm? *La historia*, the fable, is *la historia*, the history of the transculturation of the different aspects of our locus. Fernando Ortiz, an early twentieth-century Cuban ethnographer, coined the term "transculturation" to describe the historical process of identity fraught, as it was, with conquest and resistance. All of the distinct aspects of marginalized cultures become deculturated under the weight of the ever-forming ethos, "like sugar cane ground in the rollers of the mill." Instead of using the term "acculturation," the process of acquiring another culture, transculturation involves the loss or uprooting of the previous culture as it feeds the reproduction of the new phenomena (1963: 98–104). Neglecting *la historias* (the stories) of transculturation belonging to the disenfranchised makes an accurate analysis of oppression impossible.

José Martí, another Cuban philosopher, saw in the late nineteenth century the danger of the colonized adopting a Eurocentric worldview as detrimental to the existential intellectual space they occupied. He called on the oppressed of the world to create a new way of thinking based on their indigeneity. *"Nuestro vino de plátano y si es agrio es nuestro vino."* ("Let us make our wine from bananas, and if they turn out sour, it will be our wine.") To make our wine out of bananas means such a wine would naturally be sweet. But if we instead make our wine out of the fruits of Europe and it becomes sour, then we are stuck with it. Eurocentric philosophical thought sours our wine. To construct a liberative methodology upon Eurocentric philosophical paradigms is to construct resistance on shifting sand, thus contributing to our own oppression. The difficult task for the colonized is to learn how to think new thoughts in a way that is less a response and more an indigenous radical worldview different from the normative philosophies that have historically justified our subservient place within society. Rather than looking at the esteemed Eurocentric thinkers who historically wrote philosophies to purposely remove the marginalized from humanity and the fruits of liberation, we require new worldviews that resonate with the colonized.

Rejecting the reading of history through colonizer eyes—a rejection of a universal, developmental, objective, and innocent history—I consciously and unapologetically choose to privilege the *historias* (stories) of those written out of *historia* (history). And while all *historias* (histories) like *historias* (stories) are revisionist, some revisions are closer to actual events than others. Not all *historias* are equal. The "truth" of Holocaust deniers is not an equal interpretation to those who have documented the Holocaust's horrors. Employing a preferential historiographical option for those residing on the underside of history still recognizes that *historia* (story) outside *historia* (history) is nonetheless closer to actual events than the stories told to justify prevailing power structures. To create a counterhistorical narrative or story requires a methodology of gazing upon the normative dialectic and teleological history created to legitimize those whom history privileges through the eyes of those made poor, those victimized, and those made to suffer because they are relegated to the underbelly of official history. The history constructed by the intelligentsia, the affluent, and the powermongers is exchanged for the one created by those ignored by or absent from history, whose ongoing struggle is to overcome oppression.

Helpful to our analysis of Hegel's dialectic is the work of the Spanish philosopher Miguel de Unamuno who introduces the concept of *intrahistoria*, by blending objective official statistics with the monotony of the subjective everyday of ordinary real people who occupy time (what Latinx religious scholars call *lo cotidiano*[32]). *Historia* (history or story) is essentially and substantially one with *intrahistoria*, becoming a dynamic, unifying force bridging together the natural spirit with the individual (Earle 1964: 323). Unamuno's sense of history rejects all rational equations. He rails against the positivism of his day, which dismissed as irrelevant anything unproven by science and/or reason, thus dismissing the sense of mystery; for whatever was currently unknown could eventually be known as science advanced. The focus is not upon knowable grand political pacts, wars, major events, dynamic individuals, or economic forces that could be studied, measured, and analyzed. History is instead forged through unconscious acts never preserved in history books written for future generations by those whom history considered to be "nobody"—ironically, those whom Hegel removes from the movement of World History due to their inferiority.

Humans are an end, not a means. Unamuno argues, "All civilization addresses itself to man [*sic*], to each man, to each I" (1912: 67).[33] If indeed Unamuno is correct, and humans are the supreme subject of history, then I would argue that any construction of the God of History must orient history toward establishing justice by taking sides with the faceless suffering under oppression—the multiple anonymous I's of history. Eurocentric thinkers, like Hegel, frustrate our ability to establish a worldview that synchronizes with the experience of estrangement by the marginalized. Unamuno provides a paradigm of resistance to Eurocentric dominance that may be effective for the process of

---

32. *Lo cotidiano* can be understood as the everyday along with all of its particularities. As such, it can provide an interpretive lens by which the Latinx reality can be understood. María Pilar Aquino reminds us that "analysis stresses that daily life permeates the public as well as the private spheres, because the activities carried out in both spheres 'imply a level of dailiness, daily actions that confer upon this oppression, day after day, an air of naturalness'" (1993: 40). To focus on the daily existence of Latinxs is to critically analyze the good and bad shaping and forming daily life. *Lo cotidiano* incorporates the hermeneutics of the self, usually seen as unscholarly by Eurocentric thinkers. Even so, Latinx religious scholars constantly and consistently employ *lo cotidiano* in order to collapse the dichotomy between theory and praxis. In so doing, Latinx analysis is able to avoid lifeless understandings of moral dilemmas. The inclusion of Latinx everyday struggles provides a heart to the Eurocentric tendency of overemphasizing the rational. Any analytical framework indigenous to the Latinx community must therefore be unapologetically anchored in the disenfranchised autobiographical stories and testimonies. Grounding Latinx reasoning in *lo cotidiano* subverts the normalized direction of the discourse from the center toward the periphery. The everyday brings the margins to the center, and in the process challenges those accustomed to setting the parameters of ethical discourse. More than just analysis, *lo cotidiano* has the potential to become the catalyst for structural changes, serving as the foundation upon which all liberative ethical praxis is determined and implemented.
33. Unless otherwise noted in the bibliography, I have translated Unamuno's works from Spanish to English.

decolonization, namely by epitomizing the rejection of a Hegelian historical dialectical construct that actualizes Northern Europe as the telos of Western civilization. Against this, and out of concern for the preservation of his own culture, Unamuno battled for an indigenous Spaniard philosophy, modeling for us today how to see with our own eyes.

Unamuno, in *The Tragic Sense of Life*, asks if "[m]aybe the disease itself is the essential condition of what we call progress, and progress itself a disease"; after all, progress, according to the Genesis creation story, emerges with original sin (1912: 73–74). Unamuno thus summons Spaniards to resist the "progress" of Northern Europe. For Unamuno, the choice was not between Europeanization or barbarism, technology or ignorance, modernity or medievalism. He argued that the kinetic principle embodied within European technological progress is not absolute, and its imposition upon Spanish culture would rob her of her essence, for reason separates us from God (who can neither be proven nor disproven). His arguments for the rejection of the Europeanization of Spain serves us as a paradigm by which the world's marginalized can also resist the continuing Europeanization of the cultures Hegel leaves out of history.

Reconciling the Irreconcilable

Finally, a note on the methodological tension of advocating a modernist concept like liberation theology within a postmodern framework. To deny all metanarratives suggests a world where no comprehensive indictment can have the power to confront or change the status quo. If history is reduced to asynchronic movement, there can be no external position that can be characterized as a universal understanding beyond history (no certainty!). Hence, no metanarrative exists to describe the present and discern the future. Or as Foucault warns:

> We know very well that, even with the best intentions, those programs become a tool, an instrument of oppression. Rousseau, a lover of freedom, was used in the French Revolution to build up a model of social oppression. Marx would be horrified by Stalinism and Leninism. . . . My role—and that is too emphatic a word—is to show people that they are much freer than they feel. (1988: 10)

A strict embrace of Foucault can lead to a stoicism that accepts one's present social location. Acceptance fails to challenge present systems of oppression by seducing the disenfranchised to accept their lot under the logic of "it could be worse." Such an approach is similar to the premodern view that suffering and oppression in this life prepare you for the glory to come in the next life. Such approaches hamper any attempt to seek justice. For this reason, the methodology advocated throughout this book counterbalances postmodern power analysis with a modernist liberative ethics. My "perverted" usage of Foucauldian paradigms and critiques is to reconstruct a liberationist approach to systems of oppression normalized and legitimized by hope. Reading unreadable history from its underside, not as a unified universal metanarrative but as diverse and disjointed strands, becomes a legitimate vanguard to construct a new way of gazing on and privileging those relegated to the underside of history. To make a preferential option for liberative metadiscourses requires possessing understanding of the social process. Consequently, what is and what should be remain unresolved. As Argentine political theorist Ernesto Laclau observed: "It is precisely the ontological status of the central categories of the discourse of modernity and not their content, that is at stake.... Postmodernity does not imply a change in the values of Enlightenment modernity but rather a particular weakening of their absolutist character" (1988: 32). From beyond history, a constructed liberative vision of justice attempts to transform what remains untransformable—regardless of how hopeless transformation may prove to be.

Rejecting a romanticized understanding of liberative ethics based on some hopeful salvation history, we approach God based on how the earth's disenfranchised understand the space and time they occupy before a silent God. For all too many, God is the guard in the panopticon tower. Or maybe, God is the Great Leader of political posters who always gazes with an unblinking eye at creation. Because we are always being watched by the Divine, unable to hide from the relentless gaze, we have learned to impose upon ourselves our own discipline, becoming our own dominatrix.

Religion has conditioned many of the world's disenfranchised to chalk-up their oppression as God's will, either for some unknown sin committed, or to build character for the eschatological Heaven to come. And even some from the underside who have given up on God still blame themselves for their situation—repeating the lie that either they lack the intelligence, will, or drive to succeed. Liberation becomes elusive when one's history is constructed to reinforce oneself as the cause of one's victimization. Maybe liberation begins with the telling of one's own fabled *historia* (story), one's own constructed *historia* (history), as a rejection of the legitimatized dominant history created to justify the status quo. We began this chapter agreeing on the fable that Napoleon uttered a now often-quoted quip. Let us close this chapter by quoting a witticism often attributed to Friedrich Nietzsche: "Sometimes people don't want to hear the truth because they don't want their illusions destroyed." This chapter agrees with Foucault's understanding of history, capable of infinite possibilities leading nowhere. Any attempt to look for a logical progression or some moral undergirding to history is, at the very least, a misguided venture. And yet, for many, salvation history is not only the lens by which Christians make sense of the randomness of life, but becomes the bedrock of hope. But if history is itself an illusion, how then do we come to understand salvation history?

2

———

Believing Is Seeing

Standing on a windswept bluff gently sloping toward a dry creek, one feels the tranquility of the rolling prairie. Yet looks are deceiving. If one gives ear to the stories of history's forgotten, one can feel the pain of the land; not in some metaphysical way, but by the blood of yesteryear's downtrodden crying out for justice. From central Kansas to the Rocky Mountains, from the Platte to the Arkansas rivers, these pastoral lands were once the domain of the Arapaho and Southern Cheyenne people. These serene acreages were also the scene of one of the bloodiest massacres to befall a peaceful, civilized group. Nearly seven hundred indigenous individuals, mainly women and children (only about one hundred of the camp's inhabitants were fighting-age men), were besieged by a savage and primitive people committed to unspeakable atrocities. Leading 675 to 700 soldiers in the vicious attack was Union officer Colonel John Chivington.[1]

Sand Creek is approximately 175 miles southeast of Denver, a roughly four-hour drive along the back roads. Accompanying me to the site was my colleague George "Tink" Tinker of the Osage people who served as my conversation partner for this chapter. During the four-

---

1. Chivington distinguished himself during the March 1862 Battle of Glorieta Pass in New Mexico, where he was able to cut off invading Confederate troops from their supply lines, preventing the capture of the Colorado goldfields. He was also a hellfire-and-brimstone preacher who arrived in Denver in 1860 to serve as the presiding elder of the Methodist Episcopal Church for the Rocky Mountain District.

hour drive, Tinker reminds me how it would take about ten days on horseback to make this same trip. The site of the massacre is about twenty miles northeast of the town of Eads, whose population today is less than six hundred. While all the battlefields where whites perished in service to their nation are heroically cherished and hallmarked, at the Sand Creek Massacre site a spartan reception greets the visitor.

Sand Creek marked the start of a catastrophic collapse of the Plains Indians' way of life, an unavoidable consequence of the reigning salvation history of the era known as Manifest Destiny. As the young Republic moved westward, tensions developed with the indigenous occupants of the land as white settlements disrupted their nomadic life. A treaty was signed at Fort Laramie in 1851 allowing safe passage for whites in exchange for much of the Great Plains going to Natives, thus ensuring the peace. Unfortunately for Indians, gold was discovered in the Pikes Peak and South Platte regions in 1858. Homesteaders and miners rushed into the area in violation of the treaty, while demanding the US government protect them from the very people whose land they were stealing. Complicating the situation was the secession of seven southern states from the Union in 1861, creating a demand for minerals, specifically gold, to support the Union war efforts.

To secure mining interests, the federal government organized the Colorado Territory and demanded more Indian land, thus reducing the allocated land of the 1851 treaty to a fraction in 1861. Sand Creek became its northeastern corner. Few Indians agreed to this massive reduction in territory. Most, specifically the Northern Cheyenne who participated in the first outbreaks of hostility, refused to relinquish any more territory. Those who settled in Sand Creek and signed the new treaty provided "legal" justification for white land ownership, "ownership" of land they invaded and never paid for. Adding to the volatile situation, territorial Governor John Evans aspired to statehood for Colorado. To obtain his political objectives, he needed protected trade routes, a rail line to Denver, and a spur off the Oregon Trail along the South Platte River. But the governor faced one obstacle in achieving his goals—Indians.

In May 1863, Evans, hearing of a conference among the Cheyenne, Arapaho, and Sioux, sent word: "[I]f they went to war with the whites it would be a war of extermination to them" (Hoig 1961: 31). Punitive and preemptive expeditions into Indian territories by the US army led to retaliatory raids on stage stations and ranches during the spring and summer of 1864. Evans insisted he was unable to make peace, predicting that soon the "plains would swarm with United States soldiers." When Indian representatives (i.e., Black Kettle, White Antelope, and Bull Bear) attempted to broker peace by traveling to Camp Weld in Denver to negotiate with Evans and Colonel Chivington, their efforts were rebuffed (ibid.).[2]

If peace is what Indians sought, they would need to look to the military for protection and settle at Sand Creek, within the protected lands designated by the Treaty of 1861. In a letter written by George Bent to the commander of Fort Lyon, Edward W. Wynkoop, after the fruitless Denver peace talks, it was revealed that negotiators "told Black Kettle and the other chiefs that they could move to Fort Lyon and they would be protected." Other white officials "told Black Kettle to move [to Sand Creek] and no harm would be done them" (Kelman 2013: 36). Major Anthony, the fort commander who replaced Wynkoop, wrote to his superior General Curtis, reporting how he had instructed the Indians to remain in Sand Creek and promised that if peace could not be guaranteed, he would let them know. However, this assurance was a ploy to buy time. He ended his letter: "My intention, however, is to let matters remain dormant until troops can be sent out to take the field against all the tribes" (Hoig 1961: 125–27).

Chivington had high ambitions. "If I can get this appointment [to brigadier general]," he wrote to a supporter, "after the [Civil] war is over I can go to Congress or the U.S. Senate easy." But to obtain a brigadier general's star he needed another major victory, either against "rebels or redskins" (Halaas and Masich 2004: 121). He petitioned to create a regiment to deal with the "Indian problem." On August 12, 1864, Governor Evans received authorization from the War Department to raise a hundred-day volunteer cavalry. Billboards with the bold caption "Attention! Indian Fighters" were printed and distributed to recruit soldiers for the Third Regiment under Chivington's command. As summer months gave way to autumn, the war of extermination failed to materialize (Hoig 1961: 132). Lack of engagement with the so-called "hostiles" led the good folks of Denver to dub the Third Regiment as "the Bloodless Third." Fear developed that the one hundred days of subscription would expire with the regiment failing to draw any serious blood.

---

2. While the Indians who traveled to Denver sought a peaceful solution, others, like the Cheyenne Dog Soldiers, resisted further incursions by whites. The Dog Soldiers were renegade Cheyenne warriors outlawed from several different bands since 1837, who became the main physical opposition to white incursion (Halaas and Masich 2004: 116).

On November 14th, Chivington gave the Colorado Third marching orders. Along with three companies of the Colorado First, Chivington did not ride to engage Indians toward the northeast who refused to enter into peace with the whites. Instead he rode southeast toward those who were seeking peace and harmony. The ride was arduous, as rider and horse would disappear in snow-drifted gulches. Chivington and his men rode into Fort Lyon on November 28th; from there they marched toward Sand Creek. One official, Lieutenant Cramer, tried to intervene, reasoning with Chivington that any attack on the Indians at Sand Creek would be equivalent to murder, specifically these "same Indians that have saved our lives" (Hoig 1961: 142).

At first light on November 29th, the soldiers gathered at Sand Creek. The order was given to attack. "Take no prisoners" was Chivington's command, ensuring the execution of those who surrendered (ibid.: 167). As hundreds of blue-clad soldiers rushed toward the slaughter, Black Kettle raised the US flag and a white flag of truce in a vain attempt to signify the indigenous people's peaceful intention. Calling out to his compatriots, he reassured them not to be afraid, for the camp was under protection and they were in no danger (ibid.: 150). White Antelope bravely walked toward the galloping cavalry in hopes of establishing dialogue, only to realize they were in no mood for words. According to an article written by George Bent, a witness to the atrocities, and whose mother Owl Woman was matriarch to the Cheyenne's most prestigious kinship group, White Antelope "had been telling the Cheyenne for months that whites were good people and that peace was going to be made . . . induc[ing] many people to come to [Sand Creek], telling them that camp was under the protection of Fort Lyon and that no harm would come to them." Upon witnessing the slaughter befalling his people, White Antelope "made up his mind not to live any longer. . . . [He] stood in front of his lodge with his arms folded across his breast, singing the death song: 'Nothing lives long, Only the earth and the mountains'" (Kelman 2013: 39).

Besides scalping him, soldiers cut off White Antelope's ears and nose for souvenirs. According to Captain L. Wilson, his testicles were cut off and fashioned into a tobacco pouch (Hoig 1961: 182–83). When the blood-thirst was finally satisfied, about 165 to 200 Cheyenne and Arapaho lay dead, two-thirds of whom were women, children, and the elderly. An additional 200 were maimed or wounded. Even among savage and primitive people are those who realize basic humanity, as was the case with Captain Soule of Company D and Lieutenant Cramer of

Company G, both from First Colorado Regiment. They refused to fire upon peaceful Indians. When they protested the attack, Chivington ignored their pleas, responding "Damn any man who sympathizes with Indians. Kill and scalp all, big and little; nits make lice."[3]

Soule, who was just twenty-six, describes what he saw: "Hundreds of women and children were coming towards us getting on their knees for mercy." Major Anthony responded: "Kill the sons of bitches." Soule continues, "It was hard to see little children on their knees . . . having their brains beat out by men professing to be civilized . . . 'squaws' snatches were cut out for trophies . . . [a] woman was cut open, and a child taken out of her, and scalped. . . . You would think it impossible for white men to butcher and mutilate human beings as they did there, but every word I have told you is the truth, which they do not deny" (Kelman 2013: 23–24). George Bent recounts how the slaughterers of Sand Creek, upon their return to Denver, took "ghastly souvenirs . . . [including] tobacco bags made of pieces of skin cut from the bodies of dead Cheyenne women" (Kelman 2013: 40).

Soule paid the ultimate price for testifying against Chivington. In April 1865 he was ambushed and shot by a soldier with the Colorado Second named Squiers. Although Squiers was wounded, he managed to escape to New Mexico were he was captured by Lieutenant Cannon and returned to Denver. Cannon also testified to the atrocities he witnessed: "Going over the battleground the next day I did not see a body of man, woman, or child but was scalped, and in many instances their bodies were mutilated in the most horrible manner—men, women, and children's privates cut out. . . . I heard one man say that he had cut out a woman's private parts and had them for exhibition on a stick; . . . I also heard of numerous instances in which men cut out the private parts of females and stretched them over the saddle-bows, and wore them over their hats while riding in the ranks" (Hoig 1961: 180). Cannon was found a few months later mysteriously dead while Squiers "escaped," never to be captured again or stand trial.

As Tinker and I prepare to leave the site where this atrocity transpired, I notice a historical marker that simply and ambiguously reads: "Sand Creek 'Battle' or 'Massacre.'"

---

3. Ken Burns, producer, "The West, Episode Four (1856–1868): Death Runs Riot," Public Broadcasting System, 2001.

PART I: Creating a US-Centric Salvation History

Salvation histories are abstract constructions designed to justify atrocities against those not deemed "saved." President Lincoln had just been reelected president when the Sand Creek massacre occurred. General Sherman was marching toward the sea, and the long bloody Civil War was just months from concluding. Eyes were starting to turn toward the West. Stealing land occupied by others required divine inspiration: Land theft and murder must always be justified as either the very will of God, the progressive dialectical movement of history, or both. Almost twenty years prior to the Sand Creek Massacre, John O'Sullivan, editor of the *Democratic Review*, provided a romanticized jingoism that came to be known as Manifest Destiny. Capturing the pseudo-religious sentiment of European invasion, he wrote: "Our manifest destiny [is] to overspread the continent allotted by Providence for the free development of our yearly multiplying millions" (1845: 5). Till his dying day, Chivington, accepting salvation history in the form of Manifest Destiny, understood Sand Creek as a noble and necessary part of winning the West. As a farmer removes a stone before plowing a field, so too did Chivington see himself as removing an obstacle before the settlers' shout of "Westward ho!" (Kelman 2013: 9, 17).

As the Almighty gave Israel of old a Promised Land, so too does the God of the new Republic bestow upon Euroamericans, due to their racial superiority, a "virgin land" with a mandate to "tame the wilderness" and take possession of the entire continent. And just as the Hebrew God called for the genocide of all who stood in their way (Exod. 23:23), so too would the God of this New Israel—God's new chosen people—demand they violently take possession of the land occupied by the Canaanites going under names like Cheyenne or Arapaho. Manifest Destiny was a postmillennialist religious ideology. God's celestial kingdom would be realized after the US accomplished its apocalyptic mission of occupying the new "Promised Land," seen as the catalyst for ushering in Christ's second coming (Ahlstrom 1972: 845, 877–78).

This religious ideology took on political ramifications as Anglo-Saxons attempted to fulfill their providential mission of expanding white civilization and institutions across North America. Missouri Senator Thomas Hart Benton (1821–1851) articulates this divine mission, seeing the "white" race following the "divine command to subdue and replenish the earth" by destroying "savagery" and replacing the "wigwam" with the "Capitol," the "savage" with the "Christian," and the "red squaws" with the "white matrons" (Takaki 1993: 191). Not only must the Western Hemisphere bend its knees before the ideology of Manifest Destiny, but historical progression will eventually lead the entire world to do likewise. In 1885, influential minister and a leader of the Social Gospel Movement, Josiah Strong, saw the white race as extending Christianity, and thus salvation, throughout the world. He wrote:

> It seems to me that God, with infinite wisdom and skill, is training the Anglo-Saxon race for an hour sure to come in the world's future. . . . If I read not amiss, this powerful race will move down upon Mexico, down upon Central and South America, out upon the islands of the sea, over upon Africa and beyond. And can any one doubt that the result of this competition of races will be the "survival of the fittest"? (Smith 1963: 85–87)

But how can the people leading massacres be instruments for the world's salvation? Through gaslighting. Those who engaged in savagery must construct the other as the savage. As part of his defense for the barbarism unleashed under his command, Chivington argued that "a white man's scalp, not more than three days' old [was found] in one of the lodges." As Chivington's actions came under scrutiny, the one scalp grew to "several," hacked from "white men and women." A year later, one scalp (never produced as evidence) became nineteen, with a new twist. "A child captured at the camp ornamented with six white women's scalps" was presented in defense of the atrocities committed. And while the majority of those massacred were women, children, and the elderly, as evident by their remains, Chivington insisted during the inquisitions into the massacre that the camp contained an "unusual number of males," hinting that "the war chiefs of both nations were assembled . . . for some special purpose" (Kelman 2013: 9, 12–13).

Tinker refutes Chivington's claim about so-called "hostiles," reminding me that the village only had peace chiefs whose purpose from the start was to negotiate a truce with the white settlers. But unfortunately for them, Colorado could never become a state until the pacification (euphemism for genocide) of Indians. According to George Bent, "[T]he real causes of the Indian War on the plains were the wanton attacks made by the Colorado volunteers on friendly Indians." Bent went on to elucidate how it was not until the Sand Creek Massacre that Plains tribes recognized whites do not honor their treaties and have no qualms in the genocide of those who peacefully sought their protection (ibid.: 35).

The Second Coming

History has a telos, an end; and for Salvation History that end is Jesus, specifically his return and the establishment of his kingdom. In the United States, two major Christian views on the end of history predominate: postmillennialism and premillennialism.[4] US Christian understanding of Christ's return, from the Revolutionary War up until the Civil War, was mainly postmillennial. As the term indicates, Jesus will return after (post) a thousand years of peace on earth. Postmillennialism, a crucial theory for the emergence of Manifest Destiny, believes that as the gospel is preached and people are converted, evil would come to an end, making it possible for Jesus to return and establish his eschatological kingdom. America, as the New Jerusalem, as the city on the hill, was central to American self-understanding of its unique role in the fulfillment of the Book of Revelation.[5]

After the carnage of the Civil War, the hopeful postmillennialist's salvation history became difficult to maintain. The horrors of war led many instead to embrace an emended narrative—one that stressed human decline rather than progress as the hallmark of history nearing its terminal point (Marsden 1980: 48–55). A systematized version of premillennialism—which predicts the return of Christ to occur *before* the thousand-year kingdom heralded by Revelation—first emerges in the decade following the Civil War, introduced to the American public by John Nelson Darby as dispensationalism in the 1870s.[6]

4. It should be noted that there is also a third understanding of Jesus's return—amillennialism—which, as the name suggests, understands the thousand-year reign of God to be neither a literal thousand-year period of time nor a physically established kingdom.
5. American postmillennial fervor can be heard in the lyrics of the "Battle Hymn of the Republic": "Mine eyes have seen the glory of the coming of the Lord: He is trampling out the wine press where the grapes of wrath are stored; He hath loosed the fateful lightning of His terrible swift sword: His truth is marching on." The verse references the final cosmic battle laid out in the Book of Revelation, where an angel of the Lord is found casting grapes into "the great winepress of the wrath of God" (14:19), and where we find a description of how God's Word wields "a sharp sword" that "treads the winepress of the fierceness and wrath of Almighty God" (19:15). Postmillennialists believed the only thing preventing the second coming was slavery, and once it was abolished, Jesus would return.
6. Human history, according to Darby, can be divided into seven dispensations, namely: (1) innocence (prior to the Fall); (2) conscience (from the Fall up to the Flood); (3) human government (from the Flood to the call of Abraham); (4) promise (from the call of Abraham to the giving of the law at Mount Sinai); (5) law (from the giving of the law to the death of Christ); (6) grace (from the giving of the Spirit at Pentecost to Christ's second coming); and (7) kingdom (from the second coming of Christ to the establishment of the throne of judgment). Darby was not the first to discern meaning in history through its division into identifiable epochs. Albert Hernández, in his book *Subversive Fire* (2010: 93), reminds us that in the twelfth century, Joachim of Fiore provided a similar type of theology of history in his *Liber de Concordiae*. For Joachim, the trajectory of history evinces a tripartite division of time—epochs that correspond to the three persons of the Trinity. The first age, the era of the Father, is the historical period recounted in the Hebrew Bible; the sec-

For Darby, humanity is beyond reform and actually becomes continually more debased. The retrogression of humanity, in Darby's schema, eventuates in a turbulent and climactic period called the Tribulation. Tribulation will occur prior (pre) to Christ's imminent return when he establishes his thousand-year reign. Total world destruction is averted through God's intervention in Christ's parousia. Evil is defeated and Christ physically establishes his kingdom on earth. Darby's ideas became popular with such conservative evangelicals as D. L. Moody and C. I. Scofield. With the rise of fundamentalism as a response to the spread of secular humanism, liberal Christianity, Darwinism, and the use of biblical higher criticism, Darby's dispensationalism became a major tenet of most conservative-leaning Christians, and remains popular today as shown by the financial success of the *Left Behind* book series.

But what if Darby is wrong and the future is undetermined? After all, any future imagined (regardless of religious ideology) can be easily justified by current events. The rapture and second coming have always been but one generation away—the signs of the times always heralding the immediacy of the end. In other words, prophets have in every generation predicted the end is near. But all predictions have, of course, fallen short. The future is as arbitrary as the present. Theological concepts like dispensationalism (or predestination for that matter) become nonsensical. Salvation history—or any other form of progressive dialectical history—is crucial to the believer (be they religious or secular) because existence is not stable and secure, a truth that is uncomfortable for those who rely on hope to provide stability and security in the messiness of life. Rejecting such determinisms becomes an opportunity to those accustomed to their stability and security to join the constant instability and insecurity of those relegated to their underside—a true act of solidarity.

Rejecting the History of Christianity for the Sake of Salvation

The eschaton is held out as a promise through which we will be able to view all of history and fully understand everything, seeing how all things did indeed work for good according to God's purposes. Once Jesus returns, all of history will be comprehended. The Sand Creek

ond age, the era of the Son, is that historical period recorded in the New Testament; the third age begins with Pentecost, the outpouring of the Spirit, and the growth of the church on earth. The relationship of the three persons of the Trinity to human history in this scheme is the basis for hope, specifically redemptive hope.

Massacre, and all other historical points of sheer brutality and inhumanity, will be understood as redemptive. Hegel thought the meaning of history could only be comprehended when the fullness of history has been achieved. "When philosophy paints its grey in grey, a shape of life has grown old, and it cannot be rejuvenated, but only recognized by grey in grey of philosophy; the owl of Minerva[7] begins its flight only with the onset of dusk" (1820: 23). Only with the final decline of history will understanding reach its peak. But regardless of Hegel's assurances of understanding the past and present at the twilight of history, the past and present are not as static and as singular in meaning as he assumed.

The past remains fluid, evolving in meaning, ever changing in significance, constantly being reconstructed by those attempting to connect today's acts to yesterday's unrelated events. The past is whatever we choose to remember; and once we give this past meaning, we neatly place it in some artificial dialectical movement and label it universal historical progress. Likewise, relying on the future to understand the present is an illusion. Terry Eagleton, a literary theorist, reminds us "it is true that the future does not exist, any more than does the past; but rather as the past lives on in its effects, so the future may be present as a potential" (2015: 52). The operative word here is "may." Obviously, past acts impact current and future events, as the consequences of yesterday's action affect today's and tomorrow's reality. But the potential of a more just future is neither predetermined nor predestined.

Trajectories of action and decision do exist in the present, and can lead us to either utopia or dystopia. All too often, though, for the marginalized, the marching of time serves to justify and mask atrocities and injustices today as a necessary evil required to usher in some future salvation history, or some Enlightenment dialectic or, for the purposes of this chapter, a Manifest Destiny. Today's sins become a prerequisite for Heaven at the apocalyptic conclusion of history. Yet, regardless of how blissful Heaven may be, it falls short of legitimating the daily suffering of the world's wretched. Eagleton probably says it best: "Resurrection does not cancel the reality of crucifixion. . . . Indeed, one might claim that part of what disappears when the Christian doctrine of hope becomes the secular ideology of progress is precisely its tragic dimension" (2015: 27).

The final word of the theology of hope—a hope for the privi-

---

7. The owl of Minerva is the sacred bird of the Greek virgin goddess of wisdom Athena, who is syncretized with the Roman goddess Minerva.

leged—remains damning to those on its underside. The eschatological utopia of white theologians is death-dealing to all who live in the shadows of salvation history, where justice-based praxis is either absent or refashioned as a second act to Eurocentric universal theological concepts. For the world's disenfranchised to embrace a theology of hope, constructed independently of their real-life experiences, requires that they first deny their existential reality in exchange for the illusion of some dialectical movement toward a predominately white utopia that continues to exclude them in the here-and-now. Better to remain with one's feet planted in solidarity with the marginalized, sharing in their hopelessness, if we wish to contribute any praxis that might move beyond uplifting platitudes.

Salvation history is damning, for it attempts to provide comfort to the horrors of chaos caused by the lack of any real dialectical historical movement. Hope, as a product of salvation history (either metaphysical or material-dialectical), can be optimistically believed if we accept that the arc of history bends toward justice. But if the past and present are any guides, the existence of such an arc is an article of faith presumed without proof or evidence. Further, if salvation history is then simply an attempt by us to "see" or discern order in the midst of arbitrary chaos, Jürgen Moltmann's entire notion of a theology of hope falls apart.

For Moltmann, the modern prophet of hope, Christian hope must be central in the life of every Christian. "Under the conditions of history and in the circumstances of sin and death, the sovereignty of the crucified and risen Messiah Jesus is the only true *dominium terrae*.[8] It is to 'the Lamb' that rule over the world belongs" (1985: 227). The Christ event is not only true for Christians, but true for all of humanity because of its significance as an event of "universal eschatological salvation" (1967: 149). It matters not if the majority of humanity rejects the Christ event; they are still subjected to its consequences.

Manifest Destiny was but one manifestation of Christian subjugation enfleshed as hope. In the first sentence of the preface of his recent book *The Living God*, Moltmann betrays his triumphalism when he writes, "Early Christianity conquered the ancient world with its message about Christ" (2016: ix). The problem here is the word "conquered." Unfortunately for Indians (and ecology in general), said rule

---

8. *Dominium terrae* is a Christian anthropocentricity whereby nature is exploited and subjected to humans.

(conquest) under the sovereignty of the risen Messiah Jesus did not and has not worked out so well.

This risen Christ becomes foundational for Christian hope, specifically the Christian's hope for eternal life: "Christian hope is resurrection hope" (1967: 18). This hope is based on an eschatology anticipating the "return of Christ in universal glory, the judgment of the world and the consummation of the kingdom, the general resurrection of the dead and the new creation of all things . . . eschatology means the doctrine of Christian hope, which embraces both the object hoped for and also the hope inspired by it" (ibid.: 15). Because of this hope in God, the foundation for all universal human rights becomes human dignity as it emerges in the course of God's redemptive history (1984: 17). However, it is here that we can see the flaw in Moltmann's rooting a concept like human rights in the historical expression of a particular religion, for rather than universalizing human rights, it universalizes that religious expression (in this case Christianity). If human rights emerge from God's redemptive history as per Moltmann, are those who are excluded (especially by choice) from salvation history also outside of human rights? This may not be what Moltmann advocates; nevertheless, viewing Indian interaction with Europeans, this surely was the case. There is a certain brutality to the eschaton that Indians know all too well.

God, as the divine author of history, eliminates human responsibility from history, giving rise to peculiar theological perspectives like predestination. For a theology of hope to work, for a future pregnant with possibilities to exist, for a belief that in spite of the hopelessness of the now God's promises will be realized, God cannot stand above or outside of history as omniscient and omnipotent. Moltmann, in constructing a theodicy, departs from the traditional notion of a transcendent God, above and outside of time. In its place, Moltmann advocates for a refashioned Marxist Hegelianism—an all-knowing, all-powerful God who does nothing in the presence of the slaughter of the innocents. "As the Creator of the world, God also respects this world's space, time, and autonomous movements. The limitation of God's unending power is an act of God's power over Godself. Only God can limit God" (2016: 45).

On the underside of Moltmann's God is a divine construct that robs the marginalized of the very hope Moltmann advocates. To answer the theodicy question and in the process save God from God, God must also be limited to the process of time, subjected to and learning from time's movement.

[T]he living God does not know everything in advance, because God has no wish to do so. God waits for the response of those God has created . . . and creates possibilities for it. . . . If God is the source of the potentialities of those God has created, then God does not know in advance how those potentialities will be realized, and therefore is not responsible for their misuse." (ibid.: 50)

Even though God may be in front of us, whatever is future is as much unknown to God as it is to humans. Thus "peoples have the right," according to Moltmann, "to determine their own future" (1969: 39). Because Moltmann's God limits Godself to time and space, limitless possibilities for humans are created. Such a God is not yet complete, not fully God. Systematic theologian David P. Scaer probably said it best: "What we have in the 'theology of hope' is process philosophy dressed up in Biblical, even Fundamentalistic dress" (1970: 71).

The end to which time pushes God and humans is a theocentric utopian society. "The all-embracing vision of God and of a new creation is to be realized in concrete utopias which summon and make sense out of present initiatives for overcoming the present negatives of life" (1969: 40). Negatives of life, like Sand Creek, can never make sense, and initiatives to explain how such horrors will work for good make a mockery of the terrors that Christianity's victims have always faced. And while Moltmann may argue that the theologian is not concerned merely to supply a different *interpretation* of the world, of history and of human nature, but to *transform* them in expectation of a divine transformation; for Indians, said divine transformation has been deadly precisely because of the interpretations supplied by white theologians like Moltmann.

If the church has become irrelevant, then few options exist and what Moltmann provides is merely the illusion of a hopeful and utopian future. But if the church seeks relevance, then it must exist in solidarity with the wretched, in their hopelessness of the now. This is why Indians (and other massacred communities) find little comfort in Moltmann's eschatology. To them it is a final word explaining reality as a construct that sweeps all Christian atrocities under the rug of salvation history. How easy it is to embrace hope when our gaze moves beyond the suffering of the now for some faith claim of bliss in the future. "And at the end," Moltmann assures us, "all that remains is eternal life. That is the greatest of all reasons for hope" (2016: 185).

In spite of Moltmann's abstract concepts, we who are hopeless remain cognizant of the possibility that there might be no future resurrected utopia. Does it really matter if one exists or not? Do I choose to live my life based on a promised reward, or can my temporal existence have meaning for the short span of years I have on this earth? What if "nothing lives long, only the earth and the mountains?" I'm not necessarily rejecting some afterlife, it's that I simply don't care. This present age has too much oppression to be distracted by visions of kingdoms not yet seen. The choice to live a life committed to the gospel message of liberation (salvation) is never based on some future reward in the hereafter. It is based on the meaning and purpose that praxis toward liberation gives to my life in the here-and-now. Following the example of Jesus's ultimate act of solidarity with the least of these, demonstrated by picking up a cross and following them to crucifixion, becomes the model to emulate.

What if Moltmann simply gives us a tale to believe? Such a belief, though, has continually been deadly to those on his Eurocentric Christian margins. I appreciate his attempt to find divine order in the chaos of time. He wants to believe because "[f]uture history loses its attraction if there is no transcendent future for history as a whole" (2016: 180). But this assumes a social location where future is a given. For those without future, eschatological visions of utopia have the potential of creating an apathy that steers the oppressed from rebelling and creating the possibility of new realities. A life dedicated to solidarity with and liberation of the disenfranchised is worth living, for it creates meaning and purpose in the chaos and absurdity of history and the hopelessness of life caused by global oppressive structures. Praxis is what provides joy and fulfillment in the midst of hopelessness. Embracing hopelessness recognizes there is no time for God to either stand outside of or be limited within.

PART II: Christian Justification of the Genocidal Consequence of Salvation History

Genocide perpetrated against original land inhabitants is a concept rooted in and celebrated by the biblical text. One of the most powerful and foundational histories/stories is the Exodus, where God enters time and guides God's chosen out of slavery and toward the Promised Land. The trek of former slaves toward their liberation resonates with many who today are dispossessed. Unfortunately, usually ignored is that this Promised Land was already occupied by the Canaanites, who first had to be slaughtered before God's chosen could take possession of their land. *"[The Hebrews] enforced the ban on everything in [Jericho]: men and women; young and old; ox, sheep and donkey, massacring all of them"* (Josh 6:21). While most Christian liberationists read themselves into the story as oppressed slaves marching forth, first-nation people, like those massacred at Sand Creek, see themselves as modern-day Canaanites.

Reading the book of Joshua should cause any person of goodwill to pause. How does one claim a land already occupied? Salvation history built around possession of land fundamentally excludes those not chosen. To be outside of salvation history, outside the church, outside the grace of our Lord and Savior, is to be considered expendable. Unchosen Canaanites then and Indians today are given over to annihilation as excluded people. With their decimation, the "virgin land" is left clear for penetration. According to the text, God commanded that everything be put to death: men and women; young and old; ox, sheep, and donkey. Spears of God's people were thrust through babies. Swords lopped off the heads of children. Pregnant women were disemboweled. Families were decimated before each other's eyes. Chivington's Sand Creek Massacre was probably more faithful to the biblical text than we care to admit.[9]

Robert Allen Warrior provides a rereading of the Exodus story from the Canaanite perspective, questioning if it is an appropriate biblical model for understanding his people's struggle for dignity. He calls for a Christian reflection that places the Canaanites at the center of theological thought and considers the violence and injustice rarely mentioned in critical works on Exodus (1989: 49). Tinker's critique goes further. He argues that even though Christian missionaries who attempted to "Christianize the heathens" may have had the best of intentions, their religious endeavors contributed to the oppression of the indigenous people, eventually leading to their downfall. It is important to recognize that those who brought the gospel to Indians did so at a terrible cost.[10] Scholars like Vine Deloria Jr. are quick to remind us the con-

---

9. Some might argue the Canaanites, like the Indians at Sand Creek, worshiped false gods and did despicable things. But do Christians have a right to kill everything that does not recognize what they define as godly? Should Christians then invade and decimate all nonbelievers who in their eyes do despicable things? Think of the crusades. The Hebrews' (European) dream of religious freedom and liberation became the Canaanites' (Indians') nightmare of subjugation and genocide. Like the Canaanites before them, Indians were viewed as a people who could not be trusted, a snare to the righteous and a culture that required annihilation.

10. Individuals like Junípero Serra (Catholic) or Henry Benjamin Whipple (Protestant), heralded as defenders of the Indians, still contributed to their ultimate annihilation, in spite of their heartfelt convictions and intentions. Serra implemented a "reduction" paradigm for missionary conquest that physically separated Indians from their families and communities, while Whipple engineered

quest of Indian land by "God's chosen people" ended their liberation, understood as communal and personal harmony and balance. Hence, any discussion of liberation and freedom among indigenous people must be understood as liberation and freedom from European Christian invasion and its consequences (1973: 216).

True liberation for Indian people, Tinker tells me, begins with a firm "no" to Jesus Christ and Christianity, the source of Indian bondage. Can any student of history blame Tinker for saying no? Wouldn't you? Instead of the violent salvation history brought about by Christians, Indian scholars focus on the ceremonial structures of pre-1492 harmony and balance. A societal and political recentering of ancient ceremonies, along with their traditional communitarian value systems, returns to a worldview of an intimate connection to the whole of creation. But can Indians seek such balance and harmony if they adopt a Christianity based on Salvation History? Joshua saved his people, proving his God was stronger than the gods of the indigenous people of Canaan. Conquering the locals reinforces the universality of salvation history—applicable to all people in all places at all times. We follow a God of genocide, so why are we shocked with the genocide of Manifest Destiny? The massacre at Sand Creek?

When the History of Christianity Becomes a Liberal Macabre Trope

The Sand Creek Massacre is not an exception within Christian history, but rather the norm. The liberal theological school where Tink Tinker and I have taught, a school founded in the late 1800s on the mission of reconciling Darwin's evolutionary theories with Christian faith, had as its prize possession a book on Christian history displayed in a glass case at the entrance of the school's library for all to admire (fetish). The book, written by Johann Lorenz von Mosheim, a German Lutheran theologian who served as president of Göttingen University, is titled *Institutionum Historiae Christianae Compendium* [*History of Christianity*] published in 1752. The book, proudly on display from 1893 until sometime in 1974, was described by the local *Rocky Mountain News* in 1934 as ". . . a priceless vestment for the teachings of brotherly love" (Tinker 2014: 6). What makes the *History of Christianity*, as elucidated in the pages of this prized book interesting for our exploration, is not the words within the

the stealing of the Black Hills from the Sioux nation, bringing an end to their resistance (Tinker 1993: 42–67, 95–110).

text but the binding outside. The book was bound in the flayed and tanned skin of an Indian killed by a Quaker settler. The inside book cover has an inscription, dated September 16, 1893, that reads:

> This book was published 150 years ago and is covered with the skin of an Indian who was killed after a desperate struggle by General Morgan, proprietor of Morgantown, West Virginia and presented to my father, William Barns M.D. by the hand of General Morgan himself.

Research conducted by Tinker leads him to believe that General Daniel Morgan of the Revolutionary War was probably not the murderer of the Indian, but instead, a Quaker by the name of David or Daniel Morgan who settled in the Monongahela River valley (2014: 30). Who committed the atrocity is less important than the regularity by which such atrocities occurred. What Chivington's men did on that fateful dawn in November 1864 was not an aberration; it was the historical norm in which both conservatives and liberals participated.

"Why on earth did a faithful, educated methodist minister think this gruesome gift was appropriate for a school preparing people for christian ministry?" Tinker writes. "Why would the school have accepted the gift? . . . And finally, why did it take this institution of higher learning and christian values so long to decide the gift was inappropriate, to say the least?" (ibid.: 4). History must always be bound in the skins of those excluded from its pages. The excluded from salvation offer up their lives as living sacrifices so the chosen can live with the blessed assurance of an abundant life, an abundance made possible through the crucifixion of the excluded. What became of the *History of Christianity*? The skin that bound it was finally removed from the book. Indigenous people buried the remains in accordance with proper practices, honoring the once owner of said skin. As to the book, in the words of Tinker, "[T]he remains of the book, without its binding, are still housed in the Iliff library—with its stale odor of religious pornography" (2014: 3).

PART III: Imposing Order to the Chaos of Time

To be a Christian, for theologians like Moltmann, implies belief in a God who has determined a happy ending to the human story. The core of the gospel message is resurrection, ensuring our ultimate salvation in the eternal reign of God. This future reign, and our place within it, is secured by the actions that took place upon a cross in the first century.

Salvation history is designed to protect Christians from the apocalyptic danger of having their history come to an end. But maybe history is not on the side of Christians? Perhaps salvation history is just a wishful imposition of an orderly progression to history upon the chaos of the passage of time? What if seeing is not an objective process? What if what we see is based on what we believe?

Every so often Jesus or the Virgin Mary makes an appearance in some tortilla being cooked in some village, to be witnessed by the ignorant and the educated, the rich and the poor, the believer and nonbeliever. Take for example Enedina Mendoza of Tlalixtac de Cabrera, a small Oaxacan village in Mexico, who along with her family makes *tlayudas*, a traditional Mexican dish that uses baked, not fried, tortillas. In early June 2015, Enedina saw in one of the tortillas she baked the face of Jesus Christ looking back at her. Jesus appeared as a sign that the Mendoza family should attend the festival of Santo Guillermo. Overcome with reverence, she placed the holy bread beside a statue of Our Lady of Guadalupe on a small family altar. Jesus's appearance occurred about a month after an exorcism was conducted for the entire country by the bishop and a demonologist at the cathedral in the central city of San Luis Potosí, in hopes of casting out the demons of drug violence and crime plaguing the country.[11]

Jesus has not only appeared on tortillas, but for decades has also manifested himself on grilled cheese sandwiches, potatoes, bananas, naan bread, pancakes, pierogi, and even Cheetos. Not to be outdone, the Blessed Virgin Mary has also made appearances. On the Feast of Our Lady of Guadalupe, December 12, 2014, an image of Mary appeared on a church's hallway window at the Transfiguration Catholic Church in Marietta, Georgia. Father Fernando Molina-Restrepo captured a photo image of Mary who looked the same as when she appeared to Juan Diego in 1523. Parishioners reported a scent of roses when the image appeared. According to Fr. Molina-Restrepo, "We may never agree on why or how this image appeared on the window. The true gift to us will be in how we are inspired to be MORE: more forgiving, more accepting, more loving to those with whom we share our lives."[12]

Face pareidolia, an illusory phenomenon in which visual stimuli appear to resemble an unrelated object or person, is not only spiritually uplifting; but also economically profitable. In 2004, a decade-old

11. Cristina Arreola, "This Mexican Woman Claims She Saw Jesus' Face on a Homemade Tortilla," *Latina*, June 24, 2015.
12. Kelsey Ott, "Virgin Mary Image Seen on Georgia Church Window," CBS News, December 25, 2015.

toasted cheese sandwich (which apparently never got moldy) bearing the image of the Virgin Mary sold on eBay for $28,000. Diane Duyser, who first noticed the image in the autumn of 1994, said the sandwich brought her luck, including $70,000 in casino winnings—because, after all, nothing best captures Christian religiosity than the miracle of gambling winnings.[13]

Simulacra of religious figures appearing in food or on glass are real to the observer, who is neither delusional nor irrational. In fact, our brains are predisposed to see facial patterns in inanimate objects, according to a neurological study published in the journal *Cortex*. MRI brain-scan analysis indicates humans are hardwired to instinctually recognize contours as faces on virtually anything. "Our findings suggest that human face processing has a strong top-down component whereby sensory input with even the slightest suggestion of a face can result in the interpretation of a face" (Jiangang et al. 2014: 60). The same area of the brain (fusiform face area) that "lights up" during brain scans when faces are seen is also activated when people think they see faces that are not actually present. After showing subjects "noise images" (digital equivalent to film grain or visual distortions) containing no faces, but told the image did contain a face, 34 percent reported seeing a face. Depending on what people expect to see, parts of the brain are activated that allow them to see different images. Rather than saying "seeing is believing," the researchers suggest "believing is seeing" (Jiangang et al. 2014: 60).

If indeed our frontal cortexes generate expectations as we look at disorder and send signals to the posterior visual cortex to interpret stimuli based on what our brains expect to see, then can we also say our minds are predisposed to "see" patterns amidst the disorder of history in the hopes of making sense of the randomness of life? Do we see meaning in the sweep of history when none exists? If believing is seeing, does believing in a salvation history or a secular dialectical movement of time allow us to see some progressive upward linear movement? Just as some look at a cheese sandwich and see the Virgin Mary, do we look at the unintelligible passage of time and see the face of Jesus within salvation history? If true, then any quest for a progressive dialectical movement of history becomes a vain attempt to seek a scientific, rational, and/or philosophical explanation to a meaningless and chaotic thing we call time.

13. "Virgin Mary Toast Fetches 28,000," BBC News, November 23, 2004.

History as Random Montage

The illusion of history is an attempt to see order, and thus hope, in the midst of the horrors of humanity. We force ourselves to "see" patterns among disorder in hopes of giving meaning to chaos. Just as we see Jesus's image in a tortilla, a dialectical history is the Virgin Mary we see in the chaos we call time. While religious thinkers construct a salvation history as a way of discerning a meaningful pattern within time—arguing that history itself is divinely ordained—Enlightenment thinkers substitute the idea of progress as their own teleology.

But if history is indeed random, the ambiguity of existence becomes too much for some to bear. It is far too scary a proposition because it leaves us helpless before the uncertainty and randomness we call life—a space usually occupied by the world's marginalized, including peaceful Indians camping at Sand Creek. The hope that comes from a salvation history attempts to provide a comforting answer to the riddle of why horrible things happen to good people. Hope in a dialectical history holds on to the illusion of order till the bitter end. But if the good, the faithful, the believers who embrace salvation history meet hideous and horrific ends, what chance do those who fall short of the mark—and especially fall outside "history"—have?

Eurocentric history has normatively been a type of salvation history, a movement toward utopia. For the religious interpreter, historical events are characterized as the will of a benevolent God who gives meaning to the passage of time, helping to explain the tragedies of genocide. Indians deserved the genocidal onslaught at the hands of Christians because they chose to reject Jesus, thereby placing them outside of salvation history. The Enlightenment thinker, even while rejecting religious interpretations, still advocates a nontheistic salvation history, whether it be Adam Smith's "invisible hand" of rational economic thought or Karl Marx's materialist development of the perpetual struggle of labor and management.

But what if the salvation histories of religious and secular metahistorians are just what our minds are predisposed to see in the chaotic static of time's movement? What if what we call history, as per Michel Foucault, is just a series of unrelated and unconnected events that occur in a nonlinear, disjointed, multidimensional passage of time? The disjointedness of history has led many of us to see patterns where none exists, much like the image of Jesus on a tortilla.

Foucault focuses on how history lacks a straightforward progressive narrative; things could have been and could be different.

> For many years historians have preferred to turn their attention to long periods, as if, beneath the shifts and changes of political events, they were trying to reveal the stable, almost indestructible system of checks and balances, the irreversible process, the constant readjustments, the underlying tendencies that gather force, and are then suddenly reversed after centuries of continuity, the movements of accumulation and slow saturation, the great silent, motionless bases that traditional history has covered with a thick layer of events. (1972: 3)

History can never be understood as resembling the evolutionary. Instead, what has historical value is but the exteriority of accidents, complete reversals, and false appraisals (1984: 81).

Any attempt to elucidate some universal truth about human experience embedded in the historical movement of time is an erroneous venture that universalizes contingent ethical, moral, and political commitments. Understanding historical concepts to be independent from the Hegelian metaphysical German idealism, Foucault embraced the discontinuities of history, specifically scientific history. According to Foucault, any period of history is comprised of different and contradictory series of discourses, such that any all-encompassing concept is impossible (1984: 138–40). Instead we see the absence of any grand sweeping progressive historical movement governed by a rational teleology, and recognize that any thought system is a construct of arbitrary turns within time.

If all this is true, then I find myself disagreeing with Martin Luther King Jr., who, quoting the nineteenth-century abolitionist, Rev. Theodore Parker, often said "[t]he arc of the moral universe is long, but it bends toward justice" (1986: 52). The arc of the moral universe is *not* long, *nor does* it bends toward anything at all; because history lacks an arc, the universe is amoral, and an absence of salvation history means there is no bending toward justice. "The cosmos," according to Eagleton, "is no more intent on improvement than it is hell-bent on self-destruction" (2015: 97).

Looking for Jesus in the Tortilla of Time

Literary critic Walter Benjamin, like Foucault after him, provides a nonlinear, nonsuccessive conception of the movement of time. His skepticism about historical progress (or more accurately, the lack thereof) is evident when he retorts: "There is no document of civilization which is not at the same time a document of barbarism" (1940: 256 § VII). It's not that barbarism threatens culture, but rather culture is entangled in barbarism (1999: 167–68—N5a, 7). The earth's wretched, who have experienced the barbarism of civilization, are all too aware that no civilization has ever existed without domination and exploitation. And yet, as Benjamin argues, history is misinterpreted by historians, under the mask of "Progress," so as to legitimize the present, in spite of the piles of human wreckage it produces. Those who get to create history commodify what is remembered to justify the values and social power of those whom civilization privileges, literally writing their privileged space into the national epic. As we saw in the previous chapter, history is whatever the Kim dynasty (or Texas textbooks) says history is. And if not the Kim dynasty, then the institutional church, or the alternative facts spouted by the Trump administration. What if there is no historical movement that leads toward some secular ideal based on enlightenment and reason or some religious ideal based on some heavenly paradise? What the dominant culture sees as civilized, the marginalized see as its flip side—barbarism. Benjamin wrestles with how to redeem the past so that Progress's downtrodden can resist.

Benjamin attempts to create a new philosophical understanding of historical time that rejects progressivist interpretations by gazing upon the Paul Klee painting *Angelus Novus*. To gaze upon this angel of history is to see "an angel looking as though he is about to move away from something he is fixedly contemplating. His eyes are staring, his mouth is open, his wings are spread." For Benjamin, "This is how one pictures the angel of history. His face is turned toward the past. Where we perceive a chain of events, he sees one single catastrophe which keeps piling wreckage upon wreckage and hurls it in front of his feet" (1940: 257 § IX). The hopeless ice-cold gaze of the movement of time allows us to appreciate how grave and critical is our current situation. Human barbarism remains inevitable, where we exist in the current catastrophe and live in the Hell of the present, the now, the historical norm. "The tradition of the oppressed," Benjamin writes, "teaches us that the 'state of emergency' in which we live is not the exception but the rule" (1940: 256 § VIII). History is not a story of progression as per Hegel's imagination; it is the reality of an accumulating pile of wreckage the dialecticians call progress. The coming Second World War during Benjamin's time was not some future outside disaster threatening to violently invade Eurocentric humanity; rather it was the continuation of Benjamin's present. Hope, for Benjamin, was not what can be expected from the future, from the unfolding of history; rather, hope is what arises from the catastrophe, from the never-ending disaster of the human experience, from the now of Hell.

Benjamin searches for a non-Hegelian, nondialectical understanding of history; he argues for a historical materialism that "annihilates within itself the idea of progress." He seeks a repudiation of capitalist-based teleological triumphalist interpretations of history (1999: 460–N2, 2). The concept of humanity's historical progress, Benjamin reminds us, "cannot be sundered from the concept of its progression through a homogeneous, empty time" (1940: 261 § XIII). Progress becomes conjoined with a "homogeneous" and "empty" concept of time linked to capitalist bearings upon the experiences of time and projected into a possible future causally connected to past and present (2003: 395). Homogeneous time, empty of meaning, becomes commodified as labor and capital, and thus can be exchanged because they, along with time, are equivalent.

Noncapitalists, like indigenous people, experience time radically differently. Maybe the encounter of Indians and Europeans was less a clash of civilizations and more a clash of time and space. Deloria reminds us that native people are more concerned with the philosophical problem of space, rather than the Eurocentric concern with the philosophical problem of time: "Christians ask us to accept that there is a history. . . . [But w]henever we focus on one of the very important events of [our] line of history, we are told . . . that what happened was really just the growth of legends, folklore, and glorification, not a spectacular event. Yet these thinkers insist that a whole chronology of nonexistent events constitutes an important historical time line that is superior to any other explanation of human experience. This dilemma over the nature of history occurs and will occur whenever a religion is divorced from space and made an exclusive agent of time" (1973: 61, 120). Deloria contrasts the European temporal dimension with an Indian spatial location creating a "sacred geography." The Navajo, for example, may not know *when* the creation story took place, but they are certain from *where* (the exact mountains) they emerged (ibid.: 120–21).

Tinker explains to me how time is not tied to calendars, but to natural cycles giving meaning to moments. He argues the difficulty of reconciling the circular spatial understanding of time, where points of the past intersect with points of the present or future, thus the importance of festivals and ceremonies in balancing different cycles, to European developmental linear time where the past is just that, the past. But if time is indeed circular, as per Tinker, then the past is not relegated to the past, but continues in the spatial present and will continue in the future—not as a determinant but surely as an influence. Indians refusing to adapt to the linear progression of time become regarded as primitive—occupants of the premodern.

Relegating the colonized to the premodern erases them from modern European history. Premodern people only get to enter history when they are "discovered" by modern Europeans. Critical theorist Sami Khatib helps us understand how the nonhistory of the premodern can be actualized: "The persisting claims of past generations of the downtrodden point toward a past not only oppressed by official historiography but which, moreover, did not take place. These claims bear witness to a secret striving for redemption—a redemption that completes and thereby repeats a past that has never happened. . . . Ultimately, [Benjamin's] messianic *restitution* of history would be the full actualization of the past's lost and oppressed potentialities" (2013 § 30).

By arguing "the true is the whole," not only does Hegel erase the stories of those who do not occupy history, but just as terrifying, he makes space for war, massacres, and decimation (1807: 11). Because conflict is an essential component in the historical progression narrative, the "single catastrophe which keeps piling wreckage upon wreckage," as Benjamin notes, can be explained—if not justified—in the name of progress. War and conflict are necessary evils that move humanity forward and upward, saving those within liberal societies from becoming lazy, weak, and self-absorbed. Hegel is reconciled with the horrors deposited at the feet of the angel of history because he understands and embraces their contribution to the dialectic, to the progressive movement of history. The hope of Hegel's historical dialectic masks colonialism and the plight of those (like Indians) who have no right to occupy history. But for Benjamin, and those influenced by his work, such a notion is nauseating. Multiple and unceasing past atrocities make the claims of the inevitability of human progress difficult to maintain or sustain.

What we call progress is but a perverted version of modernity. The rise of fascism, under which Benjamin perished attempting to escape the grip of the Nazis, disproves the concept of a dialectic based on human progress. "One reason why Fascism has a chance," according to Benjamin, "is that in the name of progress its opponents treat it as a historical norm" (1940: 257 § VIII). The dialectic requires rejection, as revolution attempts to disrupt the imposed progressive movement of time. Theodor Adorno, who credits Benjamin's writing, responds to Hegel's assertion by stating: "Millions of Jews have been murdered, and this is to be seen as an interlude and not as the catastrophe itself" (1951: 55). For Benjamin (who as a German-Jew committed suicide rather than fall into the hands of the Gestapo) and Adorno, there was nothing redemptive about Nazism and no contribution that the Holocaust can ever make in the positive progression of humanity. For Adorno, Hegel (and I would add Marx) fails to wrestle with the concept of evil and its impact upon history (1951: 16–17).

Benjamin poetically counters Hegel, arguing that one is hard pressed to notice any type of progressive dialectical march toward a better human existence. The theological danger of proclaiming the lack of a dialectical history is that it debunks belief in a salvation history. In his attempt at disconnecting and debunking the divine eschaton from worldly telos, Benjamin writes, "The Kingdom of God is not the telos of the historical dynamic: it cannot be established as a goal. From the standpoint of history, it is not the goal by the terminus [Ende]" (2002: 305). From the historical standpoint that Benjamin occupied, there exists no premodern messianic kingdom or modernist utopia at the end of time. Rather than striving toward messianic kingdoms or utopias, humanity takes a more profane direction. What we call premodern (history made by God) and modern (history made by the scientifically minded human subject) cease being periods within linear history and instead become worldviews associated with certain time periods. Hence, premodernity can follow modernity or exist simultaneously, a phenomenon we very well may be witnessing with the rise of nationalism and fundamentalism within multiple political and religious traditions (evident among Christians who embrace the view that climate change and evolution are hoaxes).

Hope lulls activists into accepting the history of the oppressors, which constructs the chaos of the Holocaust, or Indian genocide, as a necessary conflict pushing humanity toward the next elevated historical stage. For example, the liberal Social Gospel advocate of the last century, Walter Rauschenbusch, considered it was destiny for the great empire of biblical Assyria to "grind up tribal nationalities of the ancient Orient. . . . [Because] we can see now that the process was inevitable and necessary for the development of a wider and higher civilization, but for those who got between the millstones, it was terror and agony" (1907: 24). Empire becomes an important arsenal in the hands of God. He writes: "[St.] Paul certainly did not regard the Empire as Satanic in character, but as a divine instrument of order and justice, a power holding the anti-Christian malignity in check. . . . Up to that time [Nero's early years] the persecution of the Christians had all proceeded from the hatred of the Jews [sic], and the strong arm of the Roman government had often served to protect the Christians from the influential malice of the Jews" (ibid.: 110). Rauschenbusch's progressive movement of history brings us empires by which the world is saved. Christianizing the empire leads to the fulfillment of salvation history: "The Church could be the best ally of the State in creating civil peace, because Christians had the highest morality, and because they alone had power over the demons who menaced the security of the Empire. As the soul holds the body together, so Christians hold the world together" (ibid.: 115). The hope of the world's redemption comes through the benevolent hands of a United States empire central to God's divine plan—an underlining assumption among today's Christian neoconservatives.

Hope, and the historical progress upon which it rests, I would argue, fosters a demobilizing conformity. Is not the historical dialectic that moves history in an upward spiral merely an optimistic construct forced on a very select history? The hope of "lesser people"—non-Europeans—becomes faithfulness to the tutelage received by those who inhabit the center of history. To counter such optimism, Walter Benjamin embraces a pessimistic outlook as a necessity to achieve political goals (1979: 238). The rejection of a religious salvation history, or a secular dialectical history, or any hybrid of the two, is an attempt to demystify the movement of time so that praxis can be constructed and implemented. For the liberationist, believing in hope by looking for Jesus in a tortilla or looking for order in the movement of time, distracts from the task of relieving the oppressiveness that the vast majority of humanity—present and historical—continues to endure.

For Benjamin, a storm blowing from Paradise has caught the *Angelus Novus* wings with such violence that the angel can no longer close his wings. "The storm irresistibly propels him into the future to which his back is turned, while the pile of debris before him grows skywards. This storm is what we call progress" (1940: 257 § IX). Recognizing the storm for what it is, free from imposing upon it salvific order, Benjamin embraces the hopelessness of the storm. This embrace is an essential condition for bringing about political change manifested as some quasi-messianic understanding of revolution as interrupting history. Benjamin's introduction of messianic nihilism is neither a theological pivot nor a secularization of a Judeo-Christian concept. "What characterizes revolutionary classes at the moment of action," he writes, "is the awareness that they are about to make the continuum of history explode" (2003: 395).

Those of us attempting to survive the maddening storm occupy messianic time by making the ethical choice to stand in solidarity with those who are perishing or have perished in the storm. This is the revolutionary moment when messianic time enters homogeneous empty time. To occupy messianic time is to provide intense meaning to praxis over and against the meaninglessness of homogeneous empty time. Ethics, in my case Christian ethics, is to revolutionarily occupy the now, rejecting the confines of linear history and disrupting the brewing storm in the name of those no longer able to participate in the disruption process so as to redeem all those whose past resistance failed. But the Christian might ask: Where is Jesus in the midst of this storm, in the midst of this called-for hopelessness? We might suggest that he is lamenting his forsakenness while nailed to a tree. Benjamin would have us look to the world's forsaken. "Not man or men [sic] but the struggling, oppressed class itself is the depository of historical knowledge" (1940: 260 § XII).

Maybe the purpose of crucifixion is not to be a symbol of comfort, but a strategy of survival. To claim discipleship in this Jesus is to embrace an ethics of hopelessness, of also being forsaken, propelling us toward praxis whose meaning and purpose are given to life in the struggle of implementing justice. There is nothing salvific about crucifixion. We are not saved through unjust suffering; although the oppressive suffering of the many who offer up their broken bodies as living sacrifices does provide abundant life for the elite few. But said suffering has no teleological purpose and makes a redemptive historical narrative absurd. The eleventh-century theologian Anselm of Canterbury would have us believe the purpose of the cross was necessary to satisfy God's anger, to serve as a substitute for us. Sinful humans could not redeem themselves before an angry God who required a blood atonement. Only a sinless God-as-human could complete the process, make restitution, and restore creation. In other words, in order to satisfy God's vanity, God's child must be humiliated, tortured, and brutally killed, rather than the true object of God's wrath, humans. Filicide is what placates an S&M God. The problem with Anselm's theology of atonement is that it casts God as the ultimate abuser, the ultimate oppressor who finds satisfaction through the domination, humiliation, and pain of God's child. For Christians from marginalized communities, the importance of the cross is not its redemptive powers, for all aspects of Christ's life, death, teachings, and resurrection are redemptive.

The importance of Jesus's crucifixion is the point when Christ chose solidarity with the world's marginalized, even unto death. Christ becomes one with the crucified people of his time, as well as with all who are crucified today on the crosses of classism, colonialism, racism, sexism, heterosexism, and religious discrimination. For Christians to die with Christ so they can also live with him means they too must find solidarity with the world's crucified people. Today's crosses are places of violence, littered with broken lives and bodies. For Walter Benjamin, hope for a salvation history whose telos is resurrection and redemption endows "every generation" with a "*weak* messianic power, a power on which the past has a claim" (2003: 389). He goes on to argue, "The Messiah comes not only as a redeemer, but he comes as the subduer of the Anti-Christs" (1940: 255). A history lacking a dialectical sequence of events saves us from a utopian telos based on an illusionary progressive lineage traceable to the past. Benjamin pursues a nonprogressivist form of hope where issue is taken with both triumphalism and defeatism. According to Eagleton, "[Benjamin] is strikingly close in some respects to the vision of Friedrich Nietzsche, who believed in the need to create a future that might redeem the horror of the past—one that, rather like Benjamin's Angel of History, would break violently into the spurious stability of the present as an explosive 'here and now'" (2015: 31).

If we are to hope against all hope, then it will be in understanding what Benjamin called the present, the "time of the now which is shot through with chips of Messianic time. . . . For every second of time was the strait gate through which the Messiah might enter" (1940: 263–64 § XVIII). Benjamin's understanding of messianic time rejects any hope in a secular progressive history leading to some utopian state of justice, equality, and love; for history has instead demonstrated piles of corpses consequential to the barbarous norm called human existence. Attempting to interrupt this unceasing carnage of Hegel's infinite progress, Benjamin creates a space by which the Messiah might enter, providing redemption not at some conclusion of history but in the torment of the now as it attempts to move toward a more egalitarian social order. Messiahs don't show up once, but erupt into particular moments or lives outside of linear progressive history; invading the here-and-now. Thus we are not alone in the midst of suffering due to oppression. To pick up one's cross and follow is a call for ultimate solidarity with those being crucified today. While hanging on crosses, at times—not always—glimpses of the Messiah, those anointed by God, accompany us in our trials and tribulations.

Maybe Captain Soule might be seen as one of these possible chips of messianic time. But before we elevate him to white savior status, regardless of the compassion he exhibited toward indigenous women and children at Sand Creek, we need to see that Soule remains committed to salvation history, specifically as expressed in Manifest Destiny. Soule makes clear that if Chivington had targeted hostiles instead of peaceful Indians, he would have fought beside his commander because the Union was sacrosanct and the West needed to be settled (Kelman 2013: 25). While messiahs might prove comforting, caution must be exhibited lest we worship false gods committed to salvation histories decimating the least among us. Such gods and such salvation histories require rejection.

How then does one develop an ethical approach to the dystopia reality of history's downtrodden and those disenfranchised today? Concepts like eternity, agape, justice, liberation, and salvation do not exist in their fullness at the conclusion of time, they exist in the essence of time. Chips of liberation may manifest themselves in the now, regardless of any reversals the future might bring. If we reject a linear evolutionary Eurocentric salvation history gently sloping toward some utopian promised future, how then should we understand and mark the passage of disjointed and disconnected time? And more importantly, where is God in this passage of disjointed and disconnected time? What do we do with the promises made by God?

3

There Is No God, Only Auschwitz

On a blistering August Bavarian afternoon, I rented an automobile and drove about twelve miles northwest of Munich to the quaint medieval town of Dachau. But my journey this day was not to visit Dachau Palace with its Renaissance ceilings or the beauty of the court's gardens dating to the sixteenth century. My pilgrimage was to bear witness to the birthplace of one of the greatest horrors to befall humanity in the twentieth century. On March 20, 1933, then Police Chief of Munich and SS commander Heinrich Himmler announced the establishment of the first concentration camp just outside of Dachau. At the time, the camp was not established to carry out the Final Solution; rather, its purpose was to incarcerate enemies and potential enemies of the state. Built on the grounds of an old World War I munition factory, the camp received in its first year of operation approximately 4,800 detainees to be held in "protective custody" (*Schutzhaft*), comprised mainly of German communists, socialists, trade unionists, and anyone who was deemed to be a political opponent of Hitler's regime.

With time, religious groups critical of Nazism were targeted and brought to Dachau, the vast majority of whom were Catholics. One barrack was reserved for just the clergy. Other inmates included homosexuals, Romas, antisocials (however Nazis defined the term) and criminals.[1] The camp's primary purpose was to house a surplus of forced laborers for the Nazi regime, whose only cost would be the substandard meal given. The inmates' first task was to tear down the old munition factory and build thirty-two barracks to house prisoners. They also laid down roads, drained marshes, and worked in gravel pits, and more importantly, armament production with the beginning of military hostilities. Toward the end of the war, over thirty satellite camps existed under Dachau jurisdiction, with over 30,000 prisoners exclusively working on armaments.

The first non-Germans to arrive at the camp were Austrians in March 1938, following the annexation of their country. The first Jewish prisoners, about 10,000 men, arrived at Dachau in the aftermath of *Kristallnacht*, which occurred November 9–10, 1938; although there is no doubt that Jews were among previously interned communists, socialists, and trade unionists, as well as convicted criminals. These Jewish prisoners, who had already experienced a gradual stripping of their citizenship starting in 1935 with the Nuremberg Laws, could expect worse treatment than their fellow inmates. Nevertheless, most of these Jews were released within a few months, after proving their intent to self-deport and their willingness to leave behind all earthly possessions during expatriation. As sovereign nations across Europe fell under the Nazi war machine, citizens from over thirty countries, representing resistance fighters, prisoners of war, and political opponents, found themselves interned at Dachau. From 1941 to 1943, a systematic execution of Soviet soldiers (an estimated 4,000), via firing squad, was carried out at the shooting range outside of the camp, in clear violation of the Geneva Convention.

Dachau may not have been an extermination camp; nonetheless, prisoners were brutalized and tortured, as many were worked to death. One barrack was reserved for a medical research school where human experimentations were carried out. The aim of these experiments was to develop life-saving techniques for Luftwaffe pilots. Such experiments studied the effects of decompression to measure sudden loss of pressure or oxygen experienced by pilots in high-altitude jumps. Other experiments studied hypothermia to observe the effect of extreme cold on pilots shot down over frigid seas to determine possible rescue procedures. Additionally, over 1,100 prisoners were infected with malaria in hope of discovering a medical immunization procedure for soldiers fighting in areas where the threat of the disease existed. Prisoners were also infected with tuberculosis and were subjected to experi-

---

1. Sometime after 1935, anyone who finished a prison sentence after being convicted in a court of law was automatically transferred to a concentration camp.

ments to stop bleeding, while others tested drinkable seawater. And before we in the US dismiss the Nazi barbarism of conducting medical experiments on human subjects, we do well to recall our own barbarism upon black bodies at Tuskegee, where experiments paralleled the Nazis' and didn't end until the 1970s.

By the start of the Second World War, as Germany annexed more lands with large Jewish populations, the Final Solution was fully implemented. A gas chamber was built at Dachau in 1942, although there is no evidence that it was ever used in the same fashion as at official extermination camps. Jewish prisoners were instead, starting in 1941, shipped eastwards to death camps (euphemistically known as euthanasia centers) in Poland, including Auschwitz, which was built in 1940. With four gas chambers in full operation, Auschwitz at its peak liquidated up to 6,000 Jews a day with Zyklon B. It is estimated that eleven million individuals throughout Nazi Europe perished in the concentration camp system between 1933, starting at Dachau, and 1945 with the fall of the Third Reich. Six of the eleven million exterminated were Jews.

And yet, to say six million Jews were eradicated is somewhat of an abstraction, beyond the ability of most to comprehend. We fall into the trap of not seeing individuals; instead, six million becomes a mass of people where individual humanity is lost among such an unconceivable number. Abel Herzberg, a Dutch Jew who survived the Bergen-Belsen death camp, in an attempt to capture the humanity of the individual said: "There were not six million Jews murdered; there was one murder, six million times." Thomas Buergenthal, one of the youngest survivors of Auschwitz, when discussing Herzberg's statement said:

> One of the problems with the six million number is that nobody can imagine that. You cannot personalize six million. You can personalize one person. I think it expresses a reality. It is true, because each one of those souls was killed, and each one had an individuality of his own, a history, a memory, a life, and that is lost in this whole discussion when we sort of cavalierly go over and speak about six million. It's important to keep that in mind.[2]

To think of the slaughter of one individual, with a family, a story, a history, and a future cut short, multiplied six million times is to wonder about God's six million absences. God's promise to God's chosen people

2. https://www.ushmm.org/wlc/en/media_oi.php?MediaId=5603&ModuleId=10007192.

becomes highly problematic with such overwhelming proof of abandonment. And for our purposes, what happens to a hope based on God's promises when God fails to keep those promises? But as I ask these questions, my conversation partner for this chapter, Santiago Slabodsky, reminds me when he visits death camps, he realizes the killing that occurred in Auschwitz would not have been possible if not for the consequences of the colonial ventures in the Americas and throughout Africa. What was implemented in Europe against the Jews finds its roots in modernity's colonization process. His thoughts link the suffering of genocide victims under a triumphant Christianity that has claimed for itself a new chosenness. To be chosen justifies the decimation of those not chosen. According to Slabodsky: "Those who were not chosen existed to serve those who were. Here I am thinking in the broader sense also about exterminated Natives in Latin America or Africans who were made slaves. People will die in modernity because they are not chosen and as such need to either disappear or help Manifest Destiny happen. And this applies to current Latinx/African American soldiers in the U.S." These death camps, I will argue, bear witness to the failure of modernity, the failure of rational thought, the failure of science, in effect, the failure of Enlightenment, because these concepts are foundational to colonial thought.

PART I: Moltmann's Hope versus Wiesel's Contexts

The Hebrew Scriptures introduce us to YHWH, who identifies Godself in the future tense as: "I shall be what I shall be." For Jürgen Moltmann, God's name YHWH "is a wayfaring name, a name of promise that discloses a new future, a name whose truth is experienced in history inasmuch as his promise discloses its future possibilities" (1967: 30). Reacting to the prevalence of existentialist theological thought of his time, Moltmann argued for hope based in a God who keeps promises, a God with future as God's essential nature, a God who is a step ahead of humanity making all things new. God's promise both validates the gospel and assures an eternal and blissful afterlife, safeguards a future with meaning and purpose, fortifies a sense of security, provides tranquility of mind, and most importantly, secures a sense of peace in the midst of life's vicissitudes. During an interview, Moltmann spoke of his "personal relationship" with Jesus Christ. "Jesus found me when I was eighteen years old, during the Second World War, while a prisoner of war in an English prison camp. . . . Since then I live in His ever-present presence and in expectation of His future."[3] It appears God is more present in English prison camps than in Nazi death camps. Maybe it is because salvation history excludes Jews, just as it excluded Indians in the previous chapter.

What do you do when the God of liberation fails to liberates? God may have once made a promise to the Jews, but Moltmann's God of hope is a changed God. Salvation history is given over to a new chosen, no longer the Jews, but Christians. God's promises, then, are exclusively for the new chosen. Originally, God's promises to the Hebrews were achieved through the massacre of everything drawing breath upon the land of Canaan. And when God, as we discussed in the previous chapter, promised Euroamericans their own promised land, Manifest Destiny required the genocide of Native people. The indigenous people of Canaan and the US were outside of salvation history and thus their eradication was God's will for God's chosen. So, when God's chosen (Jews) face persecution and death at the hands of others (Christians), does it mean God has a new chosen? After all, Moltmann claims his God of process theology "is free to move and to change" (2016: 36).

Are Euroamericans right when they write themselves into the historical narrative as "the New Jerusalem" or the "New Israel?" The shining light upon the hill? Moltmann argues, "In faith in the gospel, [human beings] see themselves as children of God the Father. But in prayer they talk to God as they talk to their friends. . . . Wherever a person prays in Jesus' name, God is being claimed as a friend, and the request is urgently made in the name of that friendship." (2016: 124). It would seem the problem of the Jews (or any other group who rejects the Jesus of salvation history), whose prayers from death camps are not heard by the Almighty, is that they are not praying in Jesus' name. The confidence of heard prayers can lead Moltmann to exclaim that the "world is full of jubilation, for God is in this world" (2016: 200). But if God is in this world, then God stands condemned when placed on the dock. If we protect God from a guilty verdict for failing to keep God's promises because Christians replaced Jews as the chosen, then it would require victims to bear the responsibility for their predicament, for their own slaughter, for not praying in Jesus's name, which has the power to transform their prayers to an urgent request before their buddy God. Their decimation, even if they didn't evoke the name of Jesus, must not have been urgent enough. My fear with Moltmann's

---

3. Florian Berndt, "Interview [with] Jurgen Moltmann," Tentmaker, 2015 (www.tentmaker.org/biographies/moltmann.htm).

reasoning is it absolves Christians' complicity with each single Jew murdered six million times by shifting the blame upon the single Jew for not praying in Jesus' name.

For Moltmann, the Christian who is chosen experiences God as a God of promise, a God who promises to be present. This is a God who because in the past acted within history can now be relied upon to act again (1967: 20–21). God's promise is how the present is interpreted, binding the gospel to the promise, thus forging a future of hope rooted in the risen Christ. The quality of the "not-yet" of Christ's return allows the hopelessness of the now to be exchanged for the hope for which Christians have been waiting for two millennia. But the wait, especially for those grinded under the wheel of history, has lasted so long, the promise is starting to ring hollow. This theology of promise is central to the thought of God providing the answer to every possible conceivable question, regardless of the despair and angst of the present. God's promise to act in the future becomes more important than any act, or lack thereof, that might have occurred in the past. As long as God keeps God's promises to act, hope has a chance. But if Israel's entire identity is rooted in the promises of God, then we must question if God keeps God's promises. The horrors of concentration camps bear terrible witness concerning the failure of promises to materialized. Because too many bodies of the innocent have piled up to the Heavens, hope of future promises is obscured by the tang of rotting flesh ensnared in the nostrils of God and all who are repulsed by Eurocentric futuristic fantasies based on a religious ideology constructed to provide the answer to the unanswerable.

For someone like Primo Levi, an Auschwitz survivor, God's absence is less a theological question and more a political one. The terrors of his experiences led him to declare there is no God, only Auschwitz. How can we hope in God in the midst of all the Auschwitzes Christians have established throughout history? How do Christians understand God and Jesus Christ, when those called by "His" holy name have hands drenched in the blood of crusades, pogroms, inquisitions, land theft, slavery, genocide, and colonialism? What is it about Christianity, Slabodsky (and Tinker before him) forces me to ask, that allows and justifies genocide? Too much blood spilled and too many bodies exist to simply ignore what's been done in Jesus's name, in spite of the liberating message many of us might find in the biblical text.

God's Breach of Contract

I was moved to tears when I knelt before one of the red-bricked cremea-toria at Dachau, where a lit candle flickered where flames once raged. I was agitated by the ironwork over the prisoners' entrance to the camp upon which the words *Arbeit macht frei* were wrought. There exists in these words a violent kind of hope, because this hope offered to the condemned effectively kept victims self-disciplined. Hope of possible survival leads to self-policing, as discussed in the first chapter. Heads are kept low, eye contact avoided, and rebellion muzzled in the hope they might survive, even while those around them are slain. Hopeless-ness, knowing the truth that no amount of work would ever set you free, might be more merciful and liberating. Realizing one has nothing to lose might create possible survival opportunities. Or it may not. The end may very well still be death, not freedom. But at the very least, a chance might present itself for liberation; and if not, at least hold God accountable and place God on trial.

The story is told (and made into a 2008 PBS movie[4]) of Auschwitz bar-rack inmates, who while awaiting their inevitable deaths, held a rab-binical court to decide if God was guilty of abandoning God's chosen people, if God had forsaken God's promises. Earlier in the day, the inmates faced the medical examiner who separated some to his right, others to his left—a determination of whether the inmate would live or be gassed the next day to make room for incoming prisoners. They anxiously anticipate what might be their fate, not knowing who was chosen and who was not. But as they waited, three judges were selected from among the inmates to put God on trial. During the procedures, the barrack mates air theological and biblical arguments, as well as log-ical and practical considerations. Could the God of promise be guilty of breach of contract and abandonment of the covenant?

> And YHWH this day has declared you as God's own people, his treasured possession as God has promised, and you will obey all God's command-ments. If you do, God will set you in praise, fame and honor high above all the nations God has made and you will be a holy people to YHWH, as God has promised. (Deut 26:18–19)

---

4. *God on Trial* was written by Frank Cottrell Boyce and directed by Andy de Emmony in 2008. The film was based on Nobel Laureate Elie Wiesel's play (1995) by the same title.

These were common men, intellectuals, tailors, rabbis, and unbelievers, all awaiting death and destruction for no crimes committed—except being a Jew. While some may have failed to follow the ways of God, others in the camp had lived faithful lives in love for and obedience to the Torah. But amidst filth, misery, and the hopelessness of Auschwitz, they were far from the praise, fame, and honor God promised. How does one understand, let alone follow and believe in, a God of hope who fails to keep promises?

It is frequently assumed that the story of such a trial is apocryphal. Elie Wiesel, who was fifteen years old when he arrived at Auschwitz, stated during a 2008 Holocaust Educational Trust dinner in London, "I was there when God was put on trial. . . . It happened at night; there were just three people. At the end of the trial, they used the word *chayav*, rather than 'guilty.' It means 'He owes us something.'"[5] Apparently, the trial Wiesel witnessed lasted several nights, with three masters of the Talmud, Halakah, and Jewish jurisprudence holding court. Evidence was presented and debates were held (McAfee Brown 1995: vii). But even if the event failed to literally occur, no doubt those awaiting death must have brought a similar charge against a silent God. God must be held accountable for refusing to speak to those yearning for God's voice. Something. Anything. A note of solidarity. A testament of love, of accompaniment. But they hear and receive nothing. The trial, whether it occurred or not, ends with God owing us something.

Elie Wiesel's play *God on Trial*, based on the events he claimed to have witnessed, transposes what transpired in the death camp of Auschwitz to another point of Jewish persecution in history. The play is set in 1649 in a Ukrainian village, shortly after a brutal Cossack raid. Only two Jews survive: Berish the innkeeper and his daughter Hannah. When three itinerant actors arrive to perform a Purim play, Berish instead demands they place God on trial, charging God for being absent when death and evil, in the form of a pogrom, occurs and the innocent are slaughtered. In Wiesel's play, he has the innkeeper Berish voice the same questions those sitting in death camps centuries later asked, if not audibly, then silently:

> To mention God's mercy in Shamgorod [Auschwitz] is an insult. Speak of his cruelty instead. . . . I want to understand why. He is giving strength to the killers and nothing but tears and the shame of helplessness to the

---

5. See Jenni Frazer, "Wiesel: Yes, We Really Did Put God on Trial," *The Jewish Chronicle*, September 19, 2008.

victims. . . . Every man who suffers or causes suffering, every woman who is raped, every child who is tormented implicates Him. . . . Either he is responsible or He is not. If He is, then let's judge Him; if He is not, let him stop judging us. . . . [I] accuse Him of hostility, cruelty and indifference. Either He dislikes His chosen people or He doesn't care about them—period! But then, why has He chosen us—why not someone else, for a change? Either He knows what's happening to us, or He doesn't wish to know! In both cases He is . . . guilty! Yes, guilty! Would a father stand by quietly, silently, and watch his children being slaughtered? (1979: 43, 54, 125)

Christians are, of course, familiar with these words: "Who among us would hand our child a stone when they ask for bread; or a snake when they ask for fish? If we humans, who fall short of God's glory, know how to give our children what is good, how much more should our Father in Heaven give good to those who ask?" (Luke 11:11). And yet, those who remain faithful are all too often slaughtered along with the unfaithful. The horrors humanity faces indict God as being less loving and attentive than sinful parents. I hesitate to make any pronouncements as to the character of God because in the final analysis, I lack any empirical knowledge upon which to base my study. Still with all my heart and being I want to say: my God is the God of the oppressed who incarnates Godself among the least of these. I want to make this bold claim based on the testimony of the gospel witness. But in the midst of the dark night, I confess this hopeful belief is at best a tenet accepted by faith, lacking any means of proving the truth or falsehood of the claim. In the shadow of Auschwitz, although I am not Jewish, nonetheless I am left wondering if the precious Deity who notices the fall of a sparrow is blind to God's children crushed in the winepress. Do I dare wonder if God is the God of the oppressors?

Is God the oppressor a new concept or something the biblical text has always borne witness to, but we refuse to see it because we impose a theology of an all-good and powerful God upon the text? After all, this God instructed God's chosen (as we saw in the previous chapter) to steal the land of the indigenous people of Canaan and annihilate everything with breath, including women and children (Josh 6:21; 10:40–41). How can this bloodthirsty God be the God of the oppressed? Are the inquisitors, conquistadores, colonizers, slaveholders, and today's neoliberals, who bow their knees to the Almighty, actually more faithful to the God of the Bible than the oppressed who humbly wait for a deliverance that probably never will arrive? Does God still engage in genocide for God's new chosen? The priest in Wiesel's play seems to think so:

> God, the God of your fathers, has given up on you. That's why He handed you over to us—the servants of Christ, His Son. From now on, we shall be your masters, your rulers; we shall be your God. Why would we be invested with such powers if it were not for God, who entrusted us with a mission to you, His rebellious children? It is the will of God that we, Christians, shall be your God. (ibid.: 98)

I fully understand the trepidation of placing God on trial. I would rather follow the lead of others and say at the conclusion of time, it will all be explained and make sense. I too feel a pull toward fixing my gaze at a happy ending, joyfully proclaiming "it is well with my soul." Oh, how much more comforting it would be to proclaim, "God is good—always!" With all my heart, soul, mind, and being, I wish to become intoxicated with the simplicity of unquestionable and uncomplicated faith. But to do so would be an insult to the God in whom I claim to believe. To challenge God, to yell out in protest, to place God on trial is not the ultimate act of arrogance; rather, it is to take God seriously by crucifying our Christian-based idols for an honest appraisal of the metaphysical—whatever that might or might not be. And maybe this is the ultimate beauty of faith—to doubt, to wrestle, to curse, to question, to disbelieve, to oppose, to *joder*, and to hold accountable God in defense of God's creation. God is placed on trial, not rejected, because to reject God is to reject humanity, which is created in God's image (or is it the other way around?).

Liberating Job

Finding meaning and purpose within historical events by relegating the past and present to some divine plan or will masks multiple Christian-led atrocities. For Auschwitz to exist, God must have a dark side, refusing to hear the cry of the innocent. Or maybe this is a God who really wants to do good, but lacks the power to do anything in the face of inhumanity. Simply put, this is the theodicy question that plagues those who wish to reconcile the evils of the world with the promises offered by God. We may claim God is good and all-powerful, but as the trial of God revealed, God must either be evil or impotent or some combination of both.

Faced with such a God, it seems more rational to conclude that God does not exist; or, per Nietzsche, that God is dead and *we* have killed him (1882: 120). Maybe the question with which to wrestle is not if God is dead, or if God exists; but rather, why is it so important to hold on to this God of liberation whom we claim to believe and follow? And if we hold on to this God, on what is God's character based? Why do we embrace the upward trajectory of salvation history? Why not freely accept our responsibility, along with Nietzsche, in killing God? After all, a close reading of the biblical text presents a problematic God alien to modern Christian sensitivities.

Reading the Hebrew Bible presents us with a very disturbing picture of God's character, one that Christians systematically and purposely avoid, but recognized by most Jewish thinkers. The biblical text presents a troubling God who is the cause and author of all that is good—*and all that is evil.*[6] While Christian theologians find the idea of a God responsible for evil to be heterodoxical, the biblical witness, nonetheless, is less certain. God sending evil spirits to torment Saul (1 Sam 18:10) and Jeroboam (1 Kgs 14:10); God tempting Abraham to sacrifice his son Isaac (Gen 22:1); the God of love and forgiveness, as we have already noted, calling for genocide (Josh 6:21); God's delight in smashing the heads of infants against rocks (Ps 137:9); and God wiping out innocent children who just happened to be the firstborn without regard to their nursing mothers (Exod 11:4–5). And before we dismiss these passages as a dualistic, flawed "Old" [*sic*] Testament view that must be understood in light of the New Testament focus on love, we should remember that this Jesus of love is depicted as one day returning at the head of an army to make war and conclude the apocalypse with unprecedented slaughter and decimation (Rev 19:11–21). How can any reader of the biblical text ignore the violence of the supposedly pacifist Lord, especially a violence directed against, for whatever biased reasons, those not chosen? Yet regardless of God's darker side, the Scriptures attempt to convince us God is still worthy of our worship.

How, then, does one save God from God's darker side? Making God the absolute good requires some sort of entity to serve as the antithesis to God, representing all that is evil. Hence, Satan is constructed as the personification of evil so as to magnify God's grace while legitimizing

---

6. The prophet Isaiah describes God's darker side: "I am YHWH, and there is none to rival me. I form light and create darkness, make peace and create evil, I YHWH do all these things" (45:6–7). The prophet Amos reminds us, "If there is evil in a city, has YHWH not done it?" (Amos 3:6).

the reality and presence of evil within human history. The development of Satan, specifically during the intertestamental period, was an attempt to avoid designating God as the source of evil.[7] As it became less acceptable to claim association between God and evil elements or events, an independent evil figure had to be birthed as an adversary so as to vindicate God. If evil befalls you, you deserve it for some offense committed. But Job illustrates how evil visits the sinless.

Prior to the Babylonian influence, Satan seldom appeared in the Hebrew Bible, playing a major role only in the book of Job.[8] In this early version, Satan's character is not connected to evil spirits or demonic forces, nor does he rule over an infernal, fiery underworld. Instead, Satan occupies the position of the Accuser who attends God's divine council at God's request (1:6). As accuser, he impugns Job's motive for faithfulness by asking legitimate questions (questions we should all ask of ourselves): Does Job (or in fact, any of us) honor God because he benefits from God's protection? Is piety linked to prosperity (as per Calvinist thought)? Do we continue to trust in God in times of adversity and hopelessness? (Job 1:9–11). The real test of righteousness, Satan proposes, is continued faithfulness in the midst of hopelessness, with no promise of retributive justice or anticipation of any reward.

God, basically on a dare, decides to tempt Job—making the Almighty responsible for Job's misfortunes, including the loss of his possessions, the loss of health, and more tragic, the loss of all his children. The text is clear that Satan is unable to act independently from God; any malev-

---

7. Contrary to popular opinion, the biblical text's first introduction of Satan is not as the Prince of Darkness or an enemy of God whose primordial spiritual warfare continues to manifest itself in our times. Rather, Satan is first introduced after the Babylonian captivity when returning Jews brought with them elements of Zoroastrianism. In Babylon they adopted a dualistic spirituality and an apocalyptic understanding (specifically the cosmic battle between Good and Evil), which developed over centuries as the concept of Satan as God's archenemy. His domain becomes Hell and he is responsible, along with his dominion of demons, for all existing evil (De La Torre and Hernández 2011: 63–68).

8. The Hebrew word *śāṭān* only appears nine times as a noun and six times as a verb in the Hebrew Bible. "The *satan*," used with a definite article (*haśśāṭán*), connotes "adversary(ies)," "oppose," "accuse," "accuser(s)," and/or "slander." For example, King David, a man after God's own heart, is referred to as a *satan* (1 Sam 29:4). Even God has been referred to as a *satan* (Num. 22:22). In the Hebrew Bible, any person or any creature can be a *satan*, an adversary. At some point in Hebrew history, the concept illustrated by the word *satan* was personified into the being we have come to know as Satan. This being appears to be mentioned eighteen times throughout Hebrew Scripture, appearing in only three books: once in 1 Chronicles (21:1), three times throughout two verses in Zechariah (3:11–12), and fourteen times in the first two chapters of the book of Job. In both Zechariah and Job, the definite article is used, literally "the *satan*." It is important to note all three of these books are postexilic (after 597 BCE, when some of the Israelites returned from the Babylonian captivity). Psalm 109:6 is another possibility, but it remains ambiguous. The word "satan" in that verse could either be read as "Set a wicked person over him, and let an *accuser* stand at his right hand." Or, ". . . let *Satan* stand at his right hand." The same ambiguity can be found in the story of Balaam (Num 22:22–35).

olence Satan might cause can only occur with permission from God (1:12; 2:7). Evil visits Job with God's blessing, through God's obedient servant, Satan (De La Torre and Hernández 2011: 61–63). Can we really blame Job's wife for her advice to the righteous and holy man: "Curse God and die" (2:9)? The book of Job, like the horrors of Dachau, leaves us with the troubling question as to why evil befell a faithful person like Job, or good folks trapped under Nazi rule. To read the entire book of Job is to conclude with God's heavenly response, succinctly stated as: "Tough sh*t, because I wanted to."

As I raise these questions about our understanding of God, I can almost hear some readers of this book protest by reminding me that at the end of book, the God of promise did remain faithful to Job—restoring his health and wealth. Job fathers seven new sons and two new daughters to replace those killed by Satan *on God's authority*. But children are not property where siring new ones can simply replace the old dead ones, as with the 14,000 sheep, 6,000 camels, 1,000 oxen, and 1,000 she-donkeys that replaced the livestock Satan (again on God's authority) destroyed earlier in the narrative. As any parent who has lost a child knows, no number of additional children can ever replace the loss of just one particular child. This God of Job, like the God of Dachau, leaves us with a very sadistic and brutal God.

A Methodological Note

Before continuing with this analysis, we should pause and consider a methodological question raised by Slabodsky. Specifically, how can this book explore, with integrity, the traumas of Korea, Native people in the Americas, and now Jews trapped under Nazism, and in the next chapters look at black America and Latinxs on the US southern border? The danger for this writer is to appropriate others' traumas to provide me, and you the reader, with theological meaning. Stacey Floyd-Thomas, my conversation partner in the next chapter, reminds me: If you are going to appropriate, you have to reciprocate. A problem arises when those who benefited from the genocide make use of the trauma, replacing themselves as the victims to avoid acknowledging they are the perpetrators. Following Stacey Floyd-Thomas, Slabodsky would say, "Yes, reciprocation, but taking into account the hierarchies of people, racism has structure. So if today an Afro-American takes over the Holocaust, it is fine. If a Jew in the U.S. today takes over slavery it is a problem."

Still, realizing the connectedness of those who have suffered under the barbarism of Eurocentric Christian colonialism that Slabodsky mentioned earlier, I can never speak for those who have suffered so that I can maintain religious privilege as a Christian. The only thing that I—or any person who benefits from oppressive structures—can write with any integrity is how we derive privilege from the existing power relationships. I set out not to appropriate the stories of Jews (or Indians and Koreans, and in the last chapters, blacks and undocumented Latinxs), but to understand my complicity as a believer in a religious tradition responsible for those atrocities and to ask how I can change myself and my faith to stand in solidarity with the oppressed. While not trying to appropriate the story of others, I cannot ignore those stories either, for to do so would contribute to triumphalist theologies, à la Moltmann, and set the stage for Christian participation in the next genocidal barbarism which will, no doubt, occur.

Recognizing the concerns and pitfalls of bringing the voices of others who have suffered under Christianity into the conversation, I boldly (along with trepidation) move forward in this study by asking, how do we reconcile a loving God in whom we claim to believe with the bastard God of Dachau? And more profoundly, how do we reconcile a premodern faith in the midst of our postmodern condition? Are these contradictory positions even possible? Moltmann is correct in asserting that "God cannot be proved, neither from the cosmos nor from the depths of human experience." Our disagreement comes when he turns to revelation as God-given proof of God's existence (1967: 54). But what Moltmann calls proof, I deem Eurocentric Christian ideology. God is proven in Moltmann's mind because Moltmann says God revealed Godself in a way that only Euroamerican Christians can decipher and construct. Moltmann's circular argument prevents us from wrestling with the contradictions existing between faith (the heart) or science (the mind) as rooted within the human existential social condition.

PART II: Unamuno and the Paradox of (Un)belief

How does one believe in God's promise in the midst of a historical account whose empirical evidence makes any belief in God problematic? To curse God and die is very appealing, even though I fear nihilism. Unexamined belief fails to seriously wrestle with the reality of pain and suffering. So for Christians to speak of hope in the midst of Auschwitz's or Dachau's rationally and scientifically constructed death factories is cold-hearted, callous, and cruel. While recognizing nothing redemptive about unjust pain and suffering, we have to say that it is the wretched who have an epistemological privilege, a deeper and fuller understanding of life, because they are more in touch with their mortality. The paradox is that only by embracing the absurdity of mortality can life be experienced.

We turn again to the Spanish philosopher Miguel de Unamuno, who also wrestles with, but more importantly, embraces the paradox of human existence. Unamuno's employment of paradox creates a trickster methodology of thought that is contradictory and ambiguous. The thinker is free from the restraints of dogmatic, linear, rational thought. While the Eurocentric Enlightenment battles between the premodern faith and modern science, Unamuno attempts to harmonize these polar opposites to arrive closer to whatever truth might be. The employment of paradox can be demonstrated in his poem *La oración del ateo* (The Atheist Prayer):

> You hear my supplications, God who does not exist,
> and in your nothingness gather my complaints,
> You who never leave poor men
> without consolation of deceit. You resist not.
>
> Our prayer and our yearning you see.
> When from my mind You withdraw,
> I again remember the placid fables
> with which my love sweetened my sad nights.
>
> How great You are, my God! You are so great
> that you are nothing more than an Idea; reality it is very narrow
> as much as one tries to expand
>
> to embrace you. I suffer at your expense,
> God that does not exist, but if you were to exist
> then I also would truly exist. (1910: 359)

The paradox of an atheist who prays to nothingness to damn a nonexistent God blamed for the staggering suffering of existence captures what can never be understood by those who rely on the God of salvation history. Faith becomes the atheist's vital lie. Unamuno reveals the believing unbeliever unable to believe, nevertheless willingly choosing belief. "Even if there is no God," he argues, "we would need to invent One"; for what really is important is faith in God, and not whether God actually exists. To believe has nothing to do with reason, for to believe is to wish to believe, and to believe in God is to wish there might be a God (1912: 164, 171).

Human liberative praxis is what makes God exist. The certainty of faith and doubtfulness of reason clash to create a higher level of understanding with harmonies and contradictions. "Some may see a profound contradiction in all I am saying," Unamuno would argue:

> at times expressing a longing for everlasting life, and at other times affirming this earthly life lacks the value given it. Contradiction? But of course! Of my head that says yes and my heart that says no! Naturally there are contradictions. Who cannot recall the words of the Gospel: "Lord, I believe; help me in my disbelief." Contradictions! Naturally! Since we only live of contradictions, and by them; since life is tragedy and tragedy is perpetual struggle, without victory or its hope, life is contradiction. (ibid.: 69)

The Atheist Prayer ends dismissing the Cartesian formula by questioning the reality of I (even though the I thinks), and also questioning the reality of God. Unamuno found Descartes to be a rationalist and positivist guilty of reducing individual humans to insignificant postscripts of Eurocentric progress. René Descartes' *Cogito, ergo sum* can only mean "I think therefore I am a thinker." Primary reality is not that I think but rather that I live. Descartes presents a comic doubt that is purely theoretical and provisional, a doubt of one who is pretending to doubt without really doubting (1912: 157). Thus, Unamuno counters Descartes famous dictum with *sum, ergo cogito: soy, luego pienso*—since I am human, I am also capable of thinking. Existence is not owed to thinking because those who do not think also exists (1912: 89).

Counteracting the tendency of Eurocentric thought to transform humanity (i.e., Descartes' rational animal) into a rational abstraction, Unamuno joins an irrational mode of self-awareness (passion) with the rational. Finding harmony within this paradox moves away from objectifying the individual, which denies their particular unique and intrinsic value. While recognizing the *cogito* will not be able to fully know itself, nonetheless, Unamuno moves away from abstract rational animals, where individuals are robbed of their full humanity and thus can be manipulated to accomplish the needs for those whom social structures are designed to benefit. "For a people or a person to come to know oneself," Unamuno writes, "one must study, in one way or another, one's history . . . the eye cannot see itself apart from a mirror, and mirror of the moral man [*sic*] is his works, to which he is a son [*sic*]" (1895: 91). Just as an eye is unable to see itself without the use of a mirror, so too it is difficult for a knowing self to contemplate the act of knowing separated from intuition felt through emotions. The self becomes an expressive constituent element of physical reality viewed as an independent, indivisible, and impenetrable unit of substance.

While attaining personal awareness, the I becomes conscious of its own internal contradiction: a contradiction realizing the self as a unique living being whose desire might be eternal life but nevertheless must die. The I that thinks ceases to be a rational animal as it embraces the irrationality of passions and emotions. The sorrow, or tragedy of human life lies in this paradox. Becoming conscious of this existential contradiction, the self develops awareness of the religiously problematic dilemma wherein the self is located. Recognizing one's eternal death confirms one's individuality.

And while Unamuno embraces Hegel's dialectic formula, specifically the clash between the thesis and the antithesis, which he sees as defining and becoming each the other, he nonetheless rejects its conclusion, the synthesis serving as a new thesis. Instead of reaching a synthesis, the clash of conflicting ideas reaches a paradox. Arguing that reason is constructed upon the irrational, he dismisses Hegel's aphorism that all the rational is real and all the real is rational, writing, "Many of us, not convinced by Hegel, continue believing that the real, the really real, is irrational—that reason is constructed upon irrationalities. Hegel, a great definer, pretended to reconstruct the universe with definitions, like the artillery sergeant who said the cannon was constructed by taking a hole and encasing it in steel" (1912: 61). Hegel's absolute idealism is based on a system of antitheses, contradictions, and antinomies with Kant as its "irrational root." Kant's critical idealism is based on a religious origin endangered by reason, which he attempts to save by enlarging the limits of reason even after he dissolved it in skepticism (1912: 164).

By embracing the ambiguities, contradictions, irrationalities, and paradoxes we call life, our consciousness can be broadened to include what exists beyond the realm of Enlightenment scientific and rational thought. "It is not enough to cure the plague," Unamuno writes, "we must know how to weep. Yes, we know how to weep! Perhaps this is the supreme wisdom" (ibid.: 72). These perpetual ambiguities, contradictions, irrationalities, and paradoxes become the bases for his faith, in contradistinction to simplistic faith in a God of promise. Unamuno vindicates our existence by demythologizing both scientific and philosophical abstractions, forcing us to deal with the passionate anxiety generated by a confrontation with the tragedy of our existence.

"Science [or reason] is the cemetery of dead ideas," he writes, "even though life might arise from some of them" (ibid.: 141). Concerned that "science robs people of wisdom usually converting them into phantom beings loaded with facts," he ponders if humans are made for science or science for humans (1925: 55). "Eunuchs," he writes, "will never know esthetics applied to gorgeous women, nor will pure rationalists ever know ethics, nor will they arrive at defining happiness, which is a thing to be lived and felt, not a thing that is reasoned or defined" (1912: 150). Unamuno hesitates in elevating science or reason to the realm of philosophical truth, believing philosophy is unable to transcend its own time. Instead, it reflects the activity of a given space and justifies the power structures of that space. As such, philosophy becomes the manifestation of a historical process. And salient to the historical process of central Europe is the Enlightenment reliance on science.

Kant articulated the shift to reason in making scientific and rational thought the mediators of philosophy, which then, through ethics, provides direction for the transformation of human society. He proposes a morality based on an innate "categorical imperative"[9] that is immutable and essential. Reason combined with freedom supposedly emancipated the individual from religious authoritarianism and created a controlled space for religion within the defined boundaries of reason. Thus, he exchanged the spirit of faith for the spirit of modernity. Now faith, like science, had to be objective to be believed. But Unamuno accuses Kant of making an "immortal leap" from the *Critique of Pure Reason*, in which he subjected the traditional proofs of the existence of God to a destructive analysis, to the *Critique of Practical Reason*, in which he reconstructs God, now the God of the conscience, the Author of the moral order. This immortal leap, says Unamuno, was motivated by his immortal craving for immortality, the tragic struggle of the individual to save itself (ibid.: 60).

Faith, as defined by Unamuno, is hope, which is often choked off by knowledge or belief. The "Augustinian" synthesis of reason and faith (Athens and Jerusalem) is rejected, not negated, as faith goes beyond reason. An attempt is not made to define the nature of the Divine, but rather to demonstrate how this reality produces the divinization of the

---

9. "Act only according to that maxim by which you can at the same time will that it should become a universal law" (Kant 1785: 40).

individual. "Reason and faith," he writes, "are enemies unable to maintain one without the other. The irrational seeks to be rational, and reason can only operate on the basis of the irrational. They must support each other and be associated. But associated in the struggle, for struggle is a form of association" (ibid.: 161).

Faith is not a rational concept but an imperative of the heart hoping for immortality. "God," Unamuno writes, "is Spirit and not Idea, love and not dogma, life and not logic" (1900: 55). The "agony of Christianity" refers to the tension between his feelings for a God who is incommunicable knowledge, and the truth, which is social and collective. The kernel of his philosophy is his mystic hunger for personal immortality through an ambivalent hope for the existence of God. God's existence is not a "rational necessity but vital anguish that leads us to believe in God . . . [that is] to hunger for divinity, to feel the lack and absence of God, to wish that God may exist" (1925: 217–25). Abandoning any hope for peace and tranquility as unattainable in life, he embraces the agony of struggle, for as long as there are struggles there is life, a prerequisite for existence, thus averting death.

The rational irrationality of faith, which Unamuno embraces, creates a mutual dependency where neither heartfelt belief nor intellectually based reason can exist apart from or conquer the other. "For my part," he writes, "I do not want to make peace between my heart and my head, my faith and my reason; I would rather that they fight among themselves" (1912: 168). Unashamedly claiming to stand upon the tension created by paradoxes leads him, and the rest of us who choose to follow, to struggle as we participate in a glorious forlorn spiritual quest for unanswerable questions. "You will not be really, completely, and absolutely alone until you strip yourself of yourself, beside the Sepulcher [of Don Quixote]," he writes. "Holy Solitude!"

In *The Life of Don Quixote and Sancho*, Unamuno attempts to organize a hopeless crusade for the sepulcher of "Our Lord Don Quixote," the Spanish Christ rescuing him from "graduates, curates, barbers, canons, and dukes." This holy quest of redeeming the sepulcher from the "power of the champions of Reason," and liberating ourselves from Europe's dominating rationalism, is allegorically a search for the Sepulcher of God. "We should go look for the Sepulcher of God, and redeem it from believers, unbelievers, the atheists and deists now occupying it, and wait there, crying out in supreme despair, dissolving our hearts on tears, until God resuscitates us and saves us from nothingness" (1905: 22).

Don Quixote is a man of desperation whose soul becomes a battleground of reason and immortal desire. Our Lord Don Quixote becomes the prototype of the vitalist whose faith is based on uncertainty while his faithful sidekick Sancho is the prototype of the rationalist who doubts his own reason (1912: 170). Both our Lord Don Quixote and Sancho undertake a quixotic quest, thus illustrating an empowering way to live for those of us of little or no faith. Their adventures provide us with the opportunity to live a potent and authentic life that emerges from the hopelessness due to the tragic sense of life. The comical tragic figure Don Quixote, whose passion and death are the passion, death, and resurrection of the people, employs a mad methodology.

"There is a Quixotic philosophy and even a Quixotic metaphysics, and a Quixotic logic and Quixotic ethics, and a Quixotic sense of religion—a Quixotic Spanish Catholic religious sense" argues Unamuno. "This philosophy," he continues, "this logic, this ethics, this sense of religion, that I endeavored to outline, to suggest rather than develop in this work. To develop it rationally—no; the Quixotic madness does not consent to scientific logic" (ibid.: 326). Like Our Lord Don Quixote, we charge windmills of reason in our quest for a faith existing beyond the Eurocentric rational religious dogmas so as to overcome the agony of the tragic sense of life. Existence is affirmed rather than pursuing "objective" truth or even faith in God. In a world where death camps are legitimized within evolutionary historical progress, where genocide has been normalized throughout modernity, maybe the madness of Don Quixote is the sanest path for those seeking authenticity.

To Die (Nothingness) Is Gain

For Unamuno, the "I" in attaining self-awareness becomes cognizant of the fundamental contradiction of its own nature, between the self as a unique living being whose purpose is eternal life and the self who knows it must die. "My terror," he writes, "has been annihilation, annulment, nothingness beyond the grave" (1897: 99). He is less fearful of the physical ceasing of the body to function brought about by death or the Christian concept of a Hell comprised of eternal suffering and punishment, than he is of the inconceivable but eventual loss of consciousness (1912: 91). How can consciousness conceive its complete cosmic abyss? Cognizant of this paradox, the self develops an awareness of the religious dilemma within which it lives. Realizing the eventual obviation of one's own consciousness confirms one's existential individuality, creating an anxious yearning for "salvation" and the "faith" to obtain it. Only in knowing one's mortality, or eternal nothingness, can one's existence simultaneously embody one's life and one's death.

The individual as subject and supreme object of all philosophy is a tangible creature who is born, suffers, and dies—with the emphasis on death (ibid.: 58). Unamuno's anthropocentric view of the universe sees the human as a person *"de carne y hueso,"*[10] who as both the subject and supreme object of all philosophy, struggles to answer the unanswerable human question of what happens to one's consciousness after death. The awareness of one's mortality becomes the ontological reference point in discerning the "I," and the self's world which includes God. Building on Unamuno's premise, I argue that our "self," in a liberative act, encounters the nonexistent God, face-to-face, in the space where our life, oriented toward its own end, intersects with God's own self-realization.

Eurocentric religious thought has focused on sin, on Christ's redemptive death. But what if instead we follow Unamuno, and other Spanish thinkers and mystics, with our mortality instead of our peccadilloes being central? The distinction between Europe and the Spanish soul, as Unamuno maintained, is in how each dealt with death. He struggled with its inevitability—a grappling he claimed Europeans refused to undertake. Intensity for life due to the realization of death forces one to override logic lest it obstruct passion. Such a passionate response becomes as valid as Germanic systematic reasoning (i.e., Kant). Yet, how is the existential self, aware of its own mortality, understood? Spanish literature lacks the Eurocentric motif of wrestling with one's individual sin. One is hard pressed to find any Spanish literature corresponding to *Pilgrim's Progress*. Sin is not feared; rather, what is feared is dying in vain. Juan de la Cruz captures this:

> Death cannot be bitter to the soul that loves, for in it she finds all the sweetness and delight of love. The thought of death cannot sadden her, for she finds that gladness accompanies this thought. Neither can the thought of death be burdensome and painful to her, for death will put an end to all her sorrows and afflictions and be the beginning of all her bliss. She thinks of death as her friend and bridegroom, and at the thought of it she rejoices as she would over the thought of her betrothal and marriage, and

---

10. "Flesh and bone," a Spanish idiom for our existential humanity.

she longs for that day and that hour of her death more than earthly kings long for kingdoms and principalities. (1578: Stanza XI – 14)

Unamuno attempts to strain beyond systematic thought toward purpose and reason for the existence of complex and contradictory humans in his book-length poem *The Christ of Velázquez*. Believing philosophy lies closer to poetry than to science or Enlightenment reason, he anthropomorphizes the abstract God of theologians and philosophers. He humanizes the Divine by peering into God's dark side: "Your [Christ's] humanity brings to the darkness of God the light hidden in your core" (1920: VII). Through the use of art, Unamuno wrestles with the spiritual anguish and pain caused by a God who appears absent. He sees reality and art in a close embrace where all superior works become an expression of the existential experience molded by passion and elevated to universal legitimacy. "You [Christ] created for us the night of the soul," Unamuno writes, "as a royal mantle of eternal illusions!" (ibid.: X).

Diego Velázquez's masterpiece, *Cristo de San Plácido*,[11] like philosophy, treats an insoluble situation by presenting a point of space and time within a reality that serves as an expression of the entire world. Art becomes, along with science and ethics, indispensable to any possible solution to the tragic problem of human life. Velázquez's Christ is not a synthesis of a series of movements; rather, it is a single arrested instant in the existence of Christ, a distinct moment that captures a Christ who is always dying but never dies, self-negating but not yet empty (1912: 122). He paints time by giving eternity to that instant; thus liberating Christ from the confines of both philosophy and doctrine by transcending the ideologies of the day. In Velázquez's realistic rendition, death's hopelessness finds expression in the depiction of the incarnation, death, and expected resurrection. Immortality is achieved within the moment captured by Velázquez's paintbrush; observed by Unamuno as the paradoxical Christ, "the dead Man who does not die" (1920: IV).

Such a faith cannot be contained within a rational or logical mode of thinking. Liberation is achieved through the "failure" of Jesus's ministry as depicted in his struggle upon the cross. The "irrationality" of the cross for Unamuno became the cornerstone rejected by modernity,

---

11. *Cristo de San Plácido*, also known as *Christ on the Cross*, was completed in 1635 as an oil on canvas (248 × 169 cm). It was originally painted for the Benedictine convent of San Plácido in Madrid. Today it hangs in the Prado.

but desperately needed. The philosopher's quest for the rational justification of suffering in human existence concludes with despair and a sense of God's absence or impotence. Hopelessness offers a God within suffering. Through suffering (illustrated for Christians as the cross), both philosophy as a rational progression to ultimate truth, and theology as a systematic intellectualization of God, are crucified.

I recognize that my pivot to the madness of the cross can be problematic if it is interpreted as a symbol by which Jews or any other non-Christians may find meaning. Rejecting salvation history, as a Christian (a term I admit having difficulty defining in light of all the blood shed due to Christian evangelical zeal) I struggle to make sense of a moment that is not salvific—for there is nothing salvific about suffering—and yet remains foundational to Christian thinking. Crucifixion is thus rejected as the signification of salvation. Crucifixion ceases to be the normative vehicle by which salvation, as per Christian (particularly Evangelical) theology, is obtained. Crucifixion, as a form of terror and execution, becomes for those who freely pick up their cross, an act of solidarity with the least among us—all those who today continue to be nailed on the crosses of racism, classism, sexism, heterosexism, and anti-Semitism. The bloody Christ, along with all bodies broken on the wheel of hatred and oppression, repels, if not repulses. Moving away from Unamuno's Spanish Christ and the cult of suffering attached to it, I argue, along with many womanist scholars, there is nothing redemptive in suffering. Surely a more civilized and less gory process can be constructed by the Divine by which to redeem the world. Yet Velázquez captures the repulsion of the Christ because the artist attempts to humanize him, which in turn depicts the dehumanization of Christ's suffering. This process provides a Christ who suffered freely, not as the single basic means for salvation (which seems to sanctify filicide) but as an act of solidarity with a world that suffers—a suffering and violence experienced by the Divine.

On the cross, I would argue, Christ attains the nothingness Unamuno fears and attempts to avoid; and yet, embracing this nothingness might just save both God and self. I turn to a non-Christian, Nishida Kitaro, to assist me in understanding how this paradoxical nonsalvific point in time might be helpful in the quixotic trek toward faith. Nishida, a Buddhist philosopher and contemporary of Unamuno, argued that in knowing one's mortality or eternal nothingness one's existence can simultaneously embody one's life and one's death. The existential cognizance of one's mortality becomes the ontological reference point in developing simultaneous discernment of the self and of the self's world, which includes God (1987: 15–23, 92). The location where we recognize our life to be existentially eschatological and God's own self-realization through self-expression is the space where the self encounters God face-to-face. Yet "facing" the Absolute only intensifies the self-realization of one's mortality, for to see God face-to-face is to die.

Dying ceases to be in some future event; rather, dying is now in the existential present as a relative being before the negation or emptiness of the Absolute. This raises the paradoxical structure of the divine *kenosis*, which is the praxis of God's absolute self-negation on the cross. For Unamuno, who was influenced by Søren Kierkegaard, any attempt to work out salvation must be done in "fear and trembling"; any attempt to explicate this paradox of Christianity apart from suffering or the tension created, would be repulsive. But unlike Kierkegaard, who chose God and struggled under the strain of the infinite Divinity's imposition upon the finite mind, Unamuno's distress is rooted in his inability to choose God. Contrary to Kierkegaard's "leap of faith," Unamuno refuses to share the subjective certainty of God's existence, equating God to nothingness. He writes, "[T]he logical and rational God, the God obtained by way of negation, the absolute entity, sinks, like reality itself, into nothingness; hence pure being and pure nothing, as Hegel taught, are identical. And the heartfelt God, the God of the living, is the Universe self-personified, is the Consciousness of the Universe" (1912: 213).

I will argue, along with Juan de la Cruz, we can only encounter the absolute entity in our own self-negation, which reflects the paradox of the self-negating God. De la Cruz, whose poetry revealed mysteries rather than providing rational explanations, captured the paradox of self-negation in his *Ascent of Mount Carmel* where he wrote:

> To reach satisfaction in all, desire its possession in nothing. To come to possess all, desire the possession of nothing. To arrive at being all, desire to be nothing. To come to the knowledge of all, desire the knowledge of nothing. . . . When you turn toward something you cease to cast yourself upon the all. For to go from all to the all you must deny yourself of all in all. And when you come to the possession of the all you must possess it without wanting anything. Because if you desire to have something in all your treasure in God is not purely your all. (1618: 45)

This "negative theology" confesses the irrationality of believing in a God, a mystery that eludes human reasoning and logic; for reason, according to Unamuno, can neither prove nor disprove God, the soul, or the immortality of the soul (1912: 154).

Salvation as liberation becomes the revolutionary process arrived at through a conversion experience of God's absent presence through the self-negation of the Divine on the cross, and the self-negation of the existential self before that same cross. At the foot of the cross, the dichotomy between sacred and profane ends as Divinity makes room for humanity. Two spaces become one. The self becomes more than just "dust and ashes"; the self, through negation, becomes one with the Absolute. This fusion is irreducible, lying within the spiritual, emotional, and mystical spheres we call faith. For Juan de la Cruz, becoming one with the Absolute is "the prayer of union," the indwelling of the Spirit of God in the soul (1618: 280–81). This mystagogy is described metaphorically as a spiritual marriage between Christ and the soul, the soul possessing and being possessed by Christ. Juan de la Cruz wrote:

> The Bridegroom [Christ]: "Beneath the apple tree [the cross]: There I took you for my own, There I offered you my hand, And restored you, Where your mother was corrupted." . . . The Bride [soul]: "There he gave me his breast; There he taught me a sweet and living knowledge; And I gave myself to him, Keeping nothing back; There I promised to be his bride." (1578: Stanza 23 – 1; 27 – 2)

The ambiguities, contradictions, irrationalities, and paradoxes of life are beyond the comprehension of reason and require the emotions and passions that come with life experiences. The rational intellect only serves as an obstacle rather than a means toward union with the Divine, after the soul experiences God directly and transcends reason. Nishida calls this self-awareness "subjective logic" (1987: 25). The absoluteness of faith cannot be arrived at rationally; it can only be believed and confessed. Hence Christianity avoids relativism by applying critical approaches from the standpoint of faith achieved from inner experience. Because there exists little in religion capable of rational resolution, Unamuno looks to the mystics for valid expressions of faith. But this is not Neoplatonic or Germanic mysticism, which emphasizes the metaphysical and intellectual. Rather, it is a Spanish mysticism, which passionately hungers for inward liberation through death. In a letter to Ortega y Gasset, Unamuno wrote: "They say we do not have a scientific spirit. But ours is of a different sort. . . . If it were impossible for one nation to produce both a Descartes and a Juan de la Cruz, I would choose the latter" (Salcedo, 1956: 104).

The hopeful hopelessness I argue for is possible when rooted in a mysticism—a mysticism that invites us to de-intellectualize reality. Unamuno's work vindicates our existence by demythologizing scientific and philosophical abstractions, forcing us to deal with the passionate anxiety generated by their emphasis on the eventual obliteration of our consciousness. No longer can philosophies attempt to crystallize thought into an absolute pristine system based on objective principles. Philosophy must strain beyond its systematic thought toward its purpose and reason for existence: humans—complex humans made of *carne y hueso*.

If God can be proven, an enterprise I highly doubt, it occurs when the face of God is found on the faces of Dachau's condemned and all who are marginalized and disenfranchised today. I argue that only through the engagement of liberative praxis is the existence of God proven. But even then, if we are honest with ourselves, praxis all too often falls short in even seeing God in the midst of oppressive structures. Nevertheless, our engagement in hopeless liberative praxis in the midst of the tragic becomes a quixotic crusade even if it leads to greater internal human contradictions. I can hear the reader's reply: "All this is just a jumble of contradictions!—is it God or science?" The Eurocentric enlightened mind craves, above all else, objective truths, even though they are but theological or theoretical illusions, more often than not, based on unsubstantiated hope. But why do I personally reject the legitimized and normalized "answers" routinely given by the intellectual Eurocentric leaders of religious thought, in favor of an internal incongruency that attempts to reconcile the irreconcilable mind of reason with the heart of faith? I can only respond with Unamuno's own words: "I will spend my life struggling with this mystery, even without penetrating hope, because this struggle is my nourishment and my consolation. Yes, my consolation. I have become accustomed to taking hope from desperation itself. And let not the fools and dimwits shout: 'Paradox'" (1907: 52).

Believing in the God Who Might or Might Not Exist

Building upon Unamuno's tragic sense of life, I would argue the tragedy of the human condition might have less to do with the realization of the oblivion awaiting our consciousness, and more to do with the realization of futility. What is tragic, for those of faith, is the realization that liberation fails to materialize because God has failed to keep God's promises. And rather than wrestling with what appears to be God's dark side; we either ignore the contradiction or attempt to be God's apologist. But don't we make a mockery of God when we create a theology designed to save God from God instead of doubting God's presence and goodness?

A relationship that fails to yell and scream and curse a God for ungodly acts is a faith in denial. Upon the tension caused by science and faith, the rational and the irrational, the mind and the heart, the premodern and the modern, Unamuno constructs a contradictory understanding of a Deity who makes unkept promises, who is absent when present, who offers a cruel love. Faith in the midst of profound doubt captures the human reality of the believing unbeliever. Faith is deeper among those who struggle with the nonexistent God, than among those uncritically resting on some blessed assurance of having answers to the unanswerable. The violence of the seventeenth-century pogrom, or of the twentieth-century extermination camps, is a violence not limited to the Jews but spills over to the Divine and all of humanity.

When Wiesel recounts the trial against God that occurred in the Auschwitz barracks, he states that after the rationally based court procedures that found God guilty of acts against God's chosen, they participated in a totally irrational act: they prayed.[12] At the conclusion of the movie *God on Trial*, based on the events Wiesel described, shortly after the barrack inmates find God guilty, and those chosen are marched to the gas chamber, they cover their heads and pray. Likewise, at the end of Wiesel's book by the same title, as the villagers are breaking into the inn to murder the remaining Jews, Berish the innkeeper who demanded the trial in the first place, concludes by stating, "I lived as a Jew, and it is as a Jew that I shall die—and it is as a Jew that, with my last breath, I shall shout my protest to God! And because the end is near, I shall shout louder! Because the end is near, I'll tell Him He's more guilty than ever!" (1979: 156).

There is no hope that any will be saved. There is no hope that those not chosen might live to tell their story. There is no assurance of awaiting messianic kingdoms. There is only hopelessness. Hopelessness does not mean faithlessness. This is a faith that embraces the contradictions and ambiguities of hopelessness because it is based on the contradictions and ambiguities of being human. Such an embrace,

12. See Frazer, "Wiesel: Yes, We Really Did Put God on Trial."

I would propose, constructs a mature faith upon irrationality, anticipating the illogical and absurd resurrection of a crucified hope that awkwardly unites fact with fiction. Hopelessness engenders desperation and doubt, two needed emotions that serve as the basis for faith. And yet, believers and unbelievers who took the audacious act of placing God on trial do what is totally illogical—in the midst of their hopelessness they demonstrate their faith and pray as they march toward the gas chambers, or they defiantly embrace who they are while still remaining in heated conversation, damning God. It matters not if God hears their prayers, or if there even is a God to hear; they still pray, they still debate—not for God's sake, but for their own.

This is the faith that Unamuno points us toward, a faith demonstrated by the hopeless awaiting massacre at the hands of those who rely on God's promises. But isn't this faith I'm advocating—my faith—weak because it is based on hopelessness? Hope becomes a distraction from the reality of the massacre about to unfold, an illusion obscuring what persecution demands of us. To hope is to bury one's head in the sands of peace, making us useless to meet the inevitable struggle that is coming. To pray to a God who does not answer and may not even be present is to define one's very existence in the midst of a life that is true and terrible, over and against oppressors who have failed to achieve human actualization—as demonstrated by praying Jews being led to the slaughter by Christian Nazi overlords.

As I stroll through what was once the concentration camp of Dachau, I am cognizant that this space witnessed the unspeakable horrors that befell God's children at the hands of Christians hoping for a better, purer society and future. I become more convinced that I want nothing to do with Christian hope, the protagonist of too many atrocities conducted in its name. So do not offer me your words of hope; offer me your praxis for justice. Do not shower me with reminders of God's future promises; show me God's present grace through your loving mercy. Do not tempt me with riches of some afterlife; convince me of your sacrificial agape in the here-and-now. In the midst of unfathomable suffering, the earth's marginalized no longer need pious pontifications about rewards in some hereafter. Nor do they need their oppressors providing the answers for their salvation. What is needed is disruption of the norm to push humanity toward an unachievable justice. When there is nothing to lose, when work does not set you free, not only are multiple possibilities opened up with new opportunities for radical change unimaginable to those playing it safe; but also a venue is provided by which to get real with whatever this God signifies. I close this chapter with the words Unamuno uses to conclude his book, *The Tragic Sense of Life*. He offers an ambiguous, contradictory, paradoxical, and highly problematic blessing: "May God deny you peace, so you can attain glory!" (1912: 356).

4

(Race)ing toward a New Age of Ignorance

Imagine what would happen to a German Jew in the 1930s if she or he were to walk into an SS office to raise the consciousness of Nazi sympathizers. Or if an Arapaho Indian were to approach the US cavalry on the eve of the Sand Creek Massacre in the hope of creating dialogue. Such encounters would occur with a dominant culture bent on maintaining its power and privilege through the subjugation of their Other by whatever means necessary. In the minds of oppressors, Jews or Indians—as vermin, as heathens, as standing outside the grace of Christ—are a threat to Christianity and civilization. Now imagine an African American in the Deep South during 1920s attempting to reconcile with the Ku Klux Klan. Although the African American may be a Christian, a fellow believer in the love and mercy of Jesus, they would no doubt face the same hatred and face a similar end as the Jew or the Arapaho. As courageous and noble as such praxis would be, the end result would certainly be death. And while Christians can better justify the slaughter of non-Christians for their refusal to accept God's mercy offered on the cross by Jesus Christ, how is the slaughter of African Americans, brothers and sisters in Christ, justified? If concentration camps, as discussed in the previous chapter, question the very nature of God, then Jim and Jane Crow questions the very nature of humanity.

I traveled to Charleston to attend the first annual memorial service for the "Mother Emanuel Nine." A year before, shortly after the tragedy occurred, a service was held on June 26, attended by dignitaries, including then-President Obama who from the podium sang to an overflowing arena, "Amazing Grace." President Obama began his eulogy of Reverend and State Senator Clementa C. Pinckney, and the eight others[1] murdered in their church basement, by reminding the audience that "the Bible calls us to hope . . . to have faith in things unseen." Obama looked back at a history of slavery and Jim and Jane Crow to note struggles overcome and then looked forward toward the promised land of a better future. Although the President's eulogy may well be remembered as among the most complex and intense speeches he ever gave on modern US racism, still, his theological underpinning of US salvation history might prove problematic.

If there is neither a dialectical nor salvation history propelling us toward some hopeful utopia, as previously discussed, then the future could as easily be dismal as hopeful. All that has been accomplished in race relationships over the past few years could just as easily be rolled back with the next presidential administration. Our current trajectory seems to indicate we are standing on the precipice of a new Age of Ignorance, of which Dylann Roof, the mass murderer of the Mother Emanuel Nine, is but one of its progeny. Roof demonstrates the consequences of white America's refusal to seriously wrestle with its historical racism by taking refuge in the false construct of a postracial society.

On June 17, 2015, during the Wednesday-night Bible study held in the basement of Emanuel African Methodist Episcopal Church (known lovingly as Mother Emanuel) on Calhoun Street[2] in downtown Charleston, twenty-one-year-old Roof joined Reverend Pinckney and nine other members from his flock for the study. At thirteen, Pinckney started preaching; at eighteen, he was appointed as pastor; and at twenty-three, he was elected to the South Carolina state legislature serving an economically disenfranchised district. He was both a legislator and minister because for this particular black church (and most churches of minoritized communities), praxis (through the enactment of legislation) and preaching salvation are inseparable. President Obama, during his eulogy, captured the difference between a Eurocentric individualistic theology based on orthodoxy and the collective faith of the marginalized based on orthopraxis: "To put our faith in

---

1. The Emanuel Nine are: Cynthia Marie Graham Hurd (54), Susie Jackson (87), Ethel Lee Lance (70), Depayne Middleton-Doctor (49), Pastor Clementa C. Pinckney (41), Tywanza Sanders (26), Pastor Daniel Simmons (74), Pastor Sharonda Coleman-Singleton (45), and Myra Thompson (59).
2. The street is named in honor of John Caldwell Calhoun, former Vice-President and Senator, best known for his strong defense of slavery and political theories that paved the way for secession.

action is more than just individual salvation but about our collective salvation. To feed the hungry, clothe the naked, and house the homeless is not just a call for isolated charity but the imperative of a just society."

Roof, a white man, was welcomed to the all-black Bible study. He neither looked like nor sounded like the Bible-study participants, but it did not matter. He supposedly came to pray and was thus welcomed. According to testimony by survivors of the shooting, Roof asked for Pinckney and sat next to him. For about an hour, thirteen people, including the murderer, studied Mark 4:16–17, led by Sister Myra Thompson. During Roof's interrogation, he revealed that he almost did not go through with the attack because the Bible-study participants were so nice and accepting of him. Nonetheless, ninety seconds of mayhem began with the shooting of twenty-six-year-old Tywanza Sanders who tried to shield his eighty-seven-year-old aunt. As he shot the victims, he shouted racial epithets. By the end of the study, nine, including the pastor, had been shot with a .45-caliber Glock 41 handgun. Roof waited until the Bible-study participants began to close in prayer to commence the slaughter, in hopes—according to Roof's confession—of igniting a race war. During the 2015 eulogy of the Emanuel Nine, Reverend John Gillison said, "Someone should have told that young man! He wanted to start a race war, but he came to the wrong place."

Mother Emanuel, located in Charleston, is and continues to be an integral part of the city's history. Within walking distant sits the Old Slave Museum on the original site of a slave mart that during the mid-1800s brought slave traders from all over the country to buy and sell human cargo, making the city the nation's major slave-collecting and reselling locale. Eight of every ten wealthy Americans during the antebellum period lived in South Carolina, even though 57 percent of the population were slaves. As I visited the old slave mart, now converted into a museum, I remained cognizant that within a four-block radius from where I stood, over forty additional enclosed slave markets had once flourished. And in spite of all the talk about the New South, a few blocks from the slave mart stands the Confederate Museum honoring the heritage of slaveholders. The museum displays relics of those who defended slavery, including the original lithograph of the South Carolina ordinance of secession along with two pens used to sign the document. Half a mile away from the church is Fort Sumter, where in April 1861 the first shots of the Civil War (otherwise known as the War Between the States) occurred.

Emanuel African Methodist Episcopal Church, the oldest AME church in the south, is situated in the center of the city. Because of where the church is located, it developed a record of community organizing, playing a crucial role in the history of the city, state, and nation. The church was the site of anti-slavery activism, a stop in the Underground Railroad, a community of resistance to Jim and Jane Crow, a focal point of civil rights organizing, and part of the current Black Lives Matter movement. Booker T. Washington and Martin Luther King Jr. preached from its pulpit and Coretta Scott King led a march from the church's steps to unionized, mostly black hospital workers under the gaze of some 1,000 state troopers and national guardsmen. The church, founded in 1816, was suspected in 1822 of planning the most noted failed slave revolt. The plot was discovered when a church member, George Wilson, told his master of the scheme. Once the conspiracy was revealed, thirty-five of the church members were executed after being placed on trial, including the co-founder of the church, Denmark Vesey. In retaliation for the planned rebellion, the house of worship was burned to the ground. The church went underground after being torched, meeting in secret until 1865 to evade laws banning all-black church services. Coincidentally, the alleged slave revolt was to occur at midnight, June 16, 1822. On the 193rd anniversary of the supposed uprising, Roof carried out his massacre.

Obtaining a ticket to attend the one-year memorial service was a difficult task. Literally an hour before the event took place, I scored a ticket. After going through heavy security to hear preaching about love, I sat in the quarter-filled 5,100-seat multipurpose TD Arena for the service. I participated in prayers, songs, and calls to action against continued gun violence. Large posters of each of the Emanuel Nine stood in front of the stage with the words "Still Speaking from Eternity" written above their photos. During the three-hour service, the loudest applauses and the most vocal "Amens" occurred when demands were made for greater gun restrictions. Mayor John Tecklenburg, who spoke at the event, pointed out that "[w]ords alone, no matter how sincere or well intended, cannot be substituted for sustained and meaningful action. Can't we at least remove the availability of assault weapons from those who have broken the law?" I cannot help but be moved by what occurred here less than a year ago. This is but one more atrocity that moves us as a society farther away from any true healing. I am cognizant of how impossible it is to return to some pristine past before the genocide of indigenous peoples or Jews; before the kidnapping, rape, enslavement, and Jim and Jane Crow oppression of blacks. Centuries of violence have irrevocably marked the marginalized, making the retrieval of their former identity inconceivable.

PART 1: The Pervasive Racism in the Construction of US Exceptionalism

The rejection of a salvation history, as demonstrated in the first few chapters, maintains that history is not defined through triumphant metanarratives, but instead through the contradictory and complex untold stories and struggles of the very least among us. At one point during the eulogy, President Obama quoted Rev. Pinckney's own understanding of history: "Across the South we have a deep appreciation of history. We haven't always had a deep appreciation of each other's history." The dilemma may not be two histories, where one white and one black exists not appreciated each by the other, but only one constructed history becomes official, and as such, is foisted on everyone else. If we define history as the memory of a people, even though such a history is often composed with false memories, how do the marginalized remember a history apart from the white history inflicted upon them?

Retelling stories becomes a crucial step in resisting the false histories imposed upon marginalized communities. As Edward Said insists, "[T]he idea that resistance, far from being merely a reaction to imperialism, is an alternative way of conceiving human history" (1993: 216). Recalling ignored and forgotten histories demonstrates that the massacre at Mother Emanuel is neither a recent phenomenon nor a historical abnormality. Rather, the episode is a deep-seated recurrence traceable to the very foundation of the United States. Remembering renounces victimhood. Refusing to forget the horrors of history can bring healing. Trying to forget past traumas instead leads to emotional disorders with consequences for the individual and community. "The past will not let itself be ignored," according to clinician Brandon Hamber who argues psychological restoration and healing occur only when survivors of abuse are provided with a space to remember their suffering. To be heard contributes to a collective healing process that publicly condemns the past while attempting to prevent future violations (2003: 158–59).

Centering the history of marginality challenges the constructed official history of the dominant culture. As Frantz Fanon reminds us, "The history which [the colonizer] writes is not the history of the country which he plunders but the history of his own nation in regard to all that she skims off, all that she violates and starves" (1963: 51). Ignoring the history of those who are not white, or rewriting their story, as we saw in our first-chapter discussion of Texas textbooks, is to justify white domination in memory and in the present. As my conversation partner for this chapter—Stacey Floyd-Thomas—reminds me, it is not just a false constructed history, but also the deliberate reimagining of slavery, for example, as a form of indentured servitude or "slaves as workers."[3]

To maintain the position of subject, both the colonizer and local elite are guilty of what Homi Bhabha terms the "syntax of forgetting."[4] Nation building requires an epic tale of triumphant wars, heroic figures, and awe-inspiring achievements, elevating the dominant culture while disenfranchising the history of the Other (1994: 160–61). The histories of those who are not white serve as obstacles to the dominant culture's goal of achieving ultimate power and privilege. Hence, the stories of the oppressed are sacrificed to the history of the powerful. The US national narrative disguises the complex political forces responsible for producing official history, and suppresses in the process the racial divisions created since the first Europeans set foot in the Western Hemisphere. The dominant culture reproduces itself in history and normalizes its power by engraving its memories on both things and bodies. In effect, "The body manifests the stigmata of past experience" (Foucault 1984: 83–85).

To make a preferential historiographical option for the stories and narratives of the marginalized disrupts the self-identity created by the narrative of the dominant culture. The victors of American history have inscribed their genealogies upon the national epic. All other histories are silenced, masked, or rewritten in hope that they will be forgotten. Because the history created by whites excludes marginalized recollections, it becomes a history devoid of a real subject, for the complete truth of the Euroamerican subject is missing. This is why it becomes crucial for the dominant group to enforce forgetfulness. As Fanon explains: "[C]olonialism is not simply content to impose its rule upon the present and the future of a dominated country. Colonialism is not satisfied merely with holding a people in its grip and emptying

---

3. Manny Fernandez and Christine Hauser, "Texas Mother Teaches Textbook Company a Lesson on Accuracy," *The New York Times*, October 5, 2015.
4. Homi K. Bhabha, *The Location of Culture* (New York: Routledge, 1994), 230.

the native's brain of all form and content. By a kind of perverted logic, it turns to the past of the oppressed people, and distorts, disfigures, and destroys it. This work of devaluing pre-colonial history takes on a dialectical significance today" (1963: 210).

The success of erasing the stories of the oppressed has led those who benefit from the present power structures not only to be ignorant of the history of those whose oppression made their privilege possible, but also their own history. To make a preferential historiographical option for the marginalized is an attempt not to allow those with the power to make their subjective story objective, defining the history of the marginalized, and by extension, their humanity. Recalling forgotten history forces the ones who take their narrative as normative to view the marginalized as subjects like themselves, rather than objects within their epic tales.

But hasn't political correctness made us all aware of the genocide of indigenous populations? Or the persecutions of Jews? Or the slavery of African Americans? While we may already "know" this history, peace and justice scholar John Paul Lederach reminds us that "it is a very different social phenomenon to acknowledge [it]." To acknowledge the forgotten history of the disenfranchised requires a hearing and rehearing of their stories, a process of validating their experiences and feelings—a primary step toward healing broken relationships (1997: 26). Recognizing the existence and importance of the history of the marginalized requires acknowledging that present social structures are the end product of a history the dominant culture prefers to forget. These events may have taken place in the past, but the power and privilege squeezed out of them continue to accrue. It is specifically this refusal to attempt an accurate remembrance that contributes to hopelessness.

Roof's actions signify America is just as racist at the end of President Obama's term as it was at its start. But rather than focus on Dylann Roof and his malevolent acts in particular, it would be more productive to concentrate on what Roof signifies, and the societal norms that produced Roof, as well as all the other Roofs living within the United States. As much as we may desire to depict Roof as a demented lone wolf, he clearly signifies our society's history and the deep undercurrents that continue to ripple through American culture. The church shooting can only be understood within the historical context of US racism, and any attempt to interpret Roof's actions as an isolated racially motivated incident masks the institutional violence of white constructed history. Roof's views and actions did not arise *ex nihilo*.

To occupy white bodies is to be complicit with oppressive racist social structures; regardless of how that white body feels about people of color. It matters little if one voted for a black man, or even marched with Martin Luther King Jr. Social structures remain racist for white bodies regardless how loudly or forcefully those bodies might object. At the end of the day, in spite of protestations, the overall culture normalizes and legitimizes the power possessed by white bodies who can expect to be hired before applicants of color, be paid a higher salary, be provided with greater opportunities, and face little if no harassment by the police. Stacey Floyd-Thomas reminds me how not one shot was fired in Roof's capture, but instead, officers bought him a hamburger.[5] One need not wonder what the police response would have been if a black man had shot nine white parishioners while praying. Hence, I would argue, all with white skin pigmentation are racists (or at best recovering racists) because they depend on social structures—regardless of their anti-racist rhetoric—to be racist for them.

Learning to Be Hopeless

During the Jim and Jane Crow era, Democrats were the guardians of the South's racist social structures. The passage of the Civil Rights Act under President Johnson and the implementation of the Southern Strategy[6] under President Nixon reversed the roles of Southern society's gatekeepers. Republicans, the party of Lincoln, began to win elections by appealing to whites' racist fears. It was not a coincidence that then-presidential candidate Ronald Reagan announced his 1980 candidacy by advocating states' rights in Philadelphia, Mississippi, the site of the 1964 slaying of three civil rights activists. This is not to excuse today's Democrats from their own, more paternalistic, racist strategies. Nevertheless, during the second half of the twentieth century, Republicans (and not just Trump) mastered playing the race card to win elections better than most. The political strategy employed since Nixon is responsible for creating tension among racial groups, a tension on which the education of Dylann Roof is based. Republican initiatives since the nation elected a biracial president, such as suppressing

---

5. Todd Sumlin, "Charleston Shooting Suspect's Burger King Meal Gets National Attention," *The Charlotte Observer*, June 24, 2015.
6. The Southern Strategy was implemented during the 1968 presidential campaign by Richard Nixon. The strategy was a response to the signing of the 1964 Civil Rights Act by a Democrat, which led to defection by elected Democrats to the Republican Party. Republicans appealed to white Southerners' racism to gain political support in the Southern states.

the vote of people of color (specifically blacks) through ID registration, dismantling affirmative action, and aggressive gerrymandering to disenfranchise minority communities and protect Republican seats—all create an American race-based habitus.

A few days before the Mother Emanuel Nine were massacred, then 2016 presidential candidate Donald Trump announced his candidacy by referring to Mexican immigrants as rapists. "When Mexico sends its people they're not sending their best. . . . They're bringing drugs, they're bringing crime. They're rapists and some, I assume, are good people."[7] Trump and his apologists, in scapegoating Latinxs, contribute to the false amplification of Latinx-on-white crimes. Republican presidential politicians, mindful of the delicate balance of appealing to fearful white voters to win elections, refused to condemn or rebuke such racist comments.

Riding a stream of racist comments to the White House, the two first major appointments made by the Trump administration gave a definite nod to overtly racist groups. Stephen K. Bannon, former executive of Breitbart News (which routinely runs articles on black-on-white violence), was appointed White House strategist and senior counselor, and Jeff Sessions (previously denied a federal judgeship by a Republican-controlled Senate due to his overt racism) was nominated to be US Attorney General and head of the Justice Department. The education of all the Dylann Roofs will continue because white American voters reward politicians' racist remarks, while politicians, pandering for votes, continue in their complicity with the consequences of racism such as the heinous murders in Charleston. But the real question is not how a politician like Trump, through the use of not-so-coded racist language, was able to capture the Republican presidential nomination; but how he was able to amass a following to bring him to the very height of national power—the White House. Part of his success was to speak to a constructed history of exceptionalism accepted as true by most whites (and assimilated persons of color). This history, a narrative justifying current oppressive structures, accepted as objective and true, must be taught from generation to generation, not so much in the classroom but through all aspects of life as common knowledge.

Womanist theologian Kelly Brown Douglas argues that the American white racism responsible for Trump's victory, which is masked in the language of "exceptionalism," can be traced to the Pilgrims and Puri-

7. Alexander Burns, "Choice Words from Donald Trump, Presidential Candidate," *The New York Times*, June 16, 2015.

tans who fled England in search of freedom. They saw themselves as the descendants of an ancient Anglo-Saxon people, "free from the taint of intermarriages." As such, they genetically possessed high moral values and an "instinctive love for freedom."[8] They crossed the Atlantic—as "new Israelites"—in a divine mission to build a new religious nation true to their "exceptional" Anglo-Saxon heritage.

This understanding of exceptionalism was foundational in the thinking of the Founding Fathers who established the new Republic. They conceived their Revolution as an "Anglo-centric" divine call. With the end of slavery and the increase of immigration, non-Anglo-Saxon Europeans could learn to be white "within the space of two generations,"[9] as per President Theodore Roosevelt. According to Brown Douglas, whiteness (unattainable to non-Europeans) became the passport into the exceptional space called America. She continues, "There is simply no getting around it, the myth of Anglo-Saxon exceptionalism has shaped and continues to shape America's sense of self. It is in the very DNA of this country . . . America's exceptionalism is Anglo-Saxon exceptionalism and as such, it is ingrained in the collective consciousness of America."[10] Although Trump's political rise was not surprising to communities of color, nonetheless, it remains incongruent with the hopeful American narrative (voiced by both conservative Republicans and liberal Democrats). Trump instead cements for us the political hopelessness of the future. This hopelessness is based on a history that has shown how xenophobic Christian views have previously been the root cause of so much global genocide.

There is something terribly wrong when Christian orthodoxy has been responsible, in much of the world, for horror and misery perpetrated in the name of Jesus. There exists a US Jesus who was and continues to be silent in the face of slavery, Jim and Jane Crow, and today's colorblind racism. Modernity, US Christianity, and white supremacy are triplets. The Jesus of this white Christianity, as James Cone reminds us, is satanic. This is why the Sunday eleven-o'clock hour remains the most segregated hour of the week. Floyd-Thomas insists the cause is not segregation—the cause is that Christian blacks worship a different God than Christian whites. Whites have a simplistic Christianity rooted

8. Tacitus, *Germania*, Medieval Sourcebook: https://sourcebooks.fordham.edu/source/tacitus1.html.
9. See David B. Roediger, *Working Toward Whiteness: How America's Immigrants Became White* (New York: Basic Books, 2005), 64.
10. Kelly Brown Douglas, "Donald Trump and the "Exceptionalist" Truth about America," *Faith and Resistance in the Age of Trump*, ed. Miguel A. De La Torre (Maryknoll, NY: Orbis, 2017), 14.

in the dominion of creation and people, shrouded in a Calvinist orthodoxy that raises no qualms about packing black bodies into slave ships
christened "Jesus." They see no contradictions with a slave ship captain, in spite of the human cargo packed in the hold, penning the words
to "Amazing Grace" in the midst of a storm. Although celebrated for his
Christian insight, John Newton felt no compunction in continuing his
lucrative trade for an additional seven years. This form of evil Christianity is, in the words of Floyd-Thomas, "co-producer of an educational system writing of history."

PART II: Constructing and Forgiving the Monsters of History

It is easy to see Roof as a monster, or the Nazi concentration guards, or
Chivington's men at Sand Creek, or North Korean despots. Constructing monsters simplifies our hatred for them. But even monsters pet
dogs. It is so easy to characterize the abuser as inhuman, as lacking
any sense of loving emotions. Simple binaries of good and evil defines
those labeled evil as inhumane. Although I have no intention of excus-
ing oppressive and repressive acts committed by individuals seen as
the monsters of our world (be they Hitler, Stalin, bin Laden, or even the
political candidate from the opposing party); still, their monstrous acts
are more a product of the dominant gaze they learned and internalized
since childhood than any inherited characteristic.[11]

Those who commit great atrocities also have a capacity to love.
Take for example the observations of John Paul Lederach, a profes-
sional peacemaker trained and supported by the Mennonite Church.
He recounts a 1987 encounter that occurred at the Honduras airport in
Tegucigalpa not far from the Nicaraguan border where the US-backed
Contra War was then raging. The official line was that no Nicaraguan
Contra fighters were stationed in Honduras. But Lederach, who was on
the ground, knew better, hearing the testimonies of those displaced
or from the families of the disappeared. While waiting at the airport,
a pilot with the rank of colonel entered the terminal to wait for an
incoming flight from Costa Rica.

Lederach began to wonder about the Rambo-looking pilot. "Who is
this man? Does he really believe in what he is doing? What did he
just do on the border, this very afternoon? Whose lives did he take?
. . . Who are you picking up this time, *mi Coronel*? What mercenary

---

11. Obviously there are those who are psychopaths—a conversation beyond the scope of this discussion.

for freedom will you escort this time? . . . Is this not the very evil of the war itself? American and Honduran militaries ganging up against oppressed Nicaraguans!" (1999: 46). Knowing the evils of the Contra War, Lederach felt righteous indignation at this monster engaged in the atrocities being committed. But when the plane arrived, and as the passengers disembarked, a ten-year-old girl with leg braces supporting thin legs stumbled toward him. The colonel rushed to assist her and awkwardly led her away. For a moment, Lederach's and the colonel's eyes locked. At that moment Lederach realized, "The colonel is a father like me!" (1999: 46–47).

Lederach realized that before he could construct an enemy, a monster, he first had to dehumanize another human being; only then could he experience righteous disdain. For Lederach, an enemy is created when 1) a separation is formed where the sameness shared is replaced with the differences that exist. Who I am is defined by who I am not. The origin of enmity lies in a self-definition built on a negative projection of another. 2) A superiority of self exists over against the Other; and 3) separation and superiority lead toward dehumanization, constructing an enemy devoid of God's image (1999: 47–50).

Vilifying the enemy, making them into monsters, allows easy hatred. It can even lead us to rationally visit upon them all the violence they deserve because they are, after all, such monsters. But rather than creating enemies to hate, what would happen if we could see fellow humans in need of pity—specifically, those who have chosen the false histories justifying their atrocities? The complexity of being human holds in tension loving, tender, caring individuals who can engage in Satanic acts, manifested as unspeakable brutality toward fellow human beings. Literary theorist Terry Eagleton reminds us: "To have faith in the capacity of men and women to resist injustice is not a question of supposing that such a capacity exists. Indeed, one might accept that it exists while having not the slightest faith in its robustness" (2015: 81). It is easy to construct enemies; and yes, there do exist colonels who are responsible for much death and destruction. Probably Lederach's colonel is one, maybe he is not; we will never know. But let us assume for a moment he is responsible for orchestrating killing fields. Let us assume for a moment he is indeed an enemy of the oppressed and marginalized of the world. What is our response? Pity? Love for our enemies? Forgiveness?

Forgive and Forget?

Can forgiveness counter the hopelessness fueled by our common inhumanity? During his eulogy, President Obama said, "The alleged killer could have never anticipated the way the families of the fallen would respond when they saw him in court in the midst of unspeakable grief, with words of forgiveness." During Roof's first appearance to set bond at the Charleston County court, via video conference, several of the survivors of the shooting, along with relatives of five of the shooting victims spoke directly to Roof with an offer of forgiveness. Nadine Collier, whose mother Ethel Lance was killed in the mayhem, told Roof: "I will never talk to her ever again. I will never be able to hold her again. But I forgive you and have mercy on your soul."[12] This act of forgiveness earned the church a spot as a 2016 nominee for the Nobel Peace Prize.[13]

But not all were willing to offer forgiveness. According to Esther Lance, also a daughter of Ethel Lance, "I don't forgive him because my heart ain't there. It ain't going to be no time soon. I can't forgive him."[14] Floyd-Thomas points out how the black community is far from some monolithic agreement on forgiveness. Within one black family sharing the same blood, different opinions exist. Even the tragedy will be remembered and its consequences will be remembered differently. Dot S. Scott, president of the Charleston chapter of the NAACP, expressed concern about the offering of forgiveness. "Out of respect for the grieving family, the black community in Charleston chose not to challenge the act of forgiveness even though it did not sit well with the majority. Because no remorse was offered by Roof or his family, many found it difficult, myself included, to offer forgiveness."

At one point, Dot Scott publicly challenged judge James Gosnell Jr., who presided over Roof's bond hearing, for placing an unnecessary burden upon grieving families. Magistrate Gosnell Jr., in fact, had been reprimanded by the state Supreme Court in 2005 for telling a black defendant in 2003: "There are four kinds of people in this world: black people, white people, rednecks, and n******."[15] This same magistrate

---

12. Debbie Elliott, "How a Shooting Changed Charleston's Oldest Black Church," *All Things Considered* on National Public Broadcasting, June 8, 2016.

13. Andrew Knapp, "For Emanuel AME Church, Nobel Peace Prize Nomination a 'Phenomenal' Honor," *The Post and Courier*, February 1, 2016.

14. "Some Forgive, No One Forgets: Charleston, One Year Later," *The New York Times*, June 17, 2016.

15. Elizabeth Chuck, "Judge Who Presided over Dylann Roof's Bond Hearing Was Reprimanded for Racial Slur," NBC News, June 20, 2015.

now suggested keeping the white murderer's family in mind: "We have victims, nine of them. But we also have victims on the other side. There are victims on this young man's side of the family. No one would have ever thrown them into the whirlwind of events that they have been thrown into."[16] Ms. Scott expressed how the judge's statements are part of the problem. To ask black families to forgive the perpetrator places the burden of the event upon the grieving families—something that would not have happened if the victims were white and the murderer black. They are now the ones who must bring healing to the family of the murderer. Those suffering from unjust histories must be allowed to suffer, to grieve over what was lost and can never be restored. Rushing to forgive just days after the massacre trivializes their pain, amounting to pacification without liberation.

For Stacey Floyd-Thomas, the price of forgiveness is the cost of repentance. Christians are biblically compelled to offer forgiveness to the one who repents; but Roof's refusal to do so takes forgiveness off the table. "Because grace as unmitigated favor can only be offered by God," she tells me, "demanding the oppressed to forgive their tormentor is to make them into gods and monsters. The oppressed must at once be crucified and expected to resurrect based on the oppressor's agency." True, to be forgiven is always desirable, but as Archbishop Desmond Tutu reminds us, "If you take my pen, what good does an apology do, if you still keep my pen?" (Kidwell et al., 2002: 170).

Refusing to forgive insists that the causes of injustice must first be fully examined, named, and addressed. How power and privilege are distributed within the overall society requires preliminary examination. Not surprisingly, most beneficiaries of how society is structured do not wish to engage in such analysis. A desire exists among them not to be held accountable for their complicity with atrocities and to simply move on without limiting the very oppressive structures that continue to benefit them. The challenge for those accustomed to their privilege is how to obtain forgiveness without having to sacrifice accumulated wealth and power.

But maybe before we even begin a conversation about offering forgiveness to Roof, a need exists to forgive God for refusing to safeguard followers lifting up their prayers? One church mourner cried out, "If we're not safe in the church, God, you tell us where we are safe!"[17] But is God deaf to this mourner's query? Was God not present as two

---

16. Abby Phillip, "The Charleston Magistrate Who Sparked a Debate About Who Is a Victim," *The Washington Post*, June 21, 2015.

or more gathered? Rather than attempting to excuse God for failing to protect the faithful, it may be healthier to curse God, to cry out in anger, to demand where the hell was God as the innocent were being slaughtered in the very house of God. To vent against God places us in good company, for Moses shook his fist at God, crying out "Why have you done evil to your servant? And why have I not found grace in your sight?" (Num 11:11). Jesus, while dying on the cross, cried out in anguish from the midst of his abandonment and desertion, "My God, my God, why have you forsaken me?" (Matt 27:46). Crying out to God for failing to keep promises becomes a crucial step in learning how to be human. Denying feelings of abandonment by a God in whom we placed our faith is detrimental to our spiritual and physical health. Rather than constructing a God who exists to serve our every whim, anger toward a nonresponsive God reinforces the words of the psalmist: "For our God is in heaven: God has done whatever was pleasing to Godself" (Ps 115:3).

Salvation history may end with "the wolf dwelling with the lamb, and the leopard lying down with the goat" (Isa 11:6); but in the meantime, the lamb and the goat will not get a good night's rest. We are left wondering about the wisdom of lambs and goats forgiving wolves and leopards for what is their nature. Offering forgiveness may prove deadly. We are reminded of Nietzsche's "bird of prey" comment to the lambs: "we don't dislike them at all, these good little lambs; we even love them: nothing is more tasty than a tender lamb" (1887: 1:13). After more than half a millennium where black lives don't matter, has forgiveness for centuries of slaughter only emboldened the birds of prey? Utopias present us with a Heaven where whites and blacks might live in peace; but in the meantime, blacks have also learned to sleep with one eye open, doing everything possible to maintain a safe distance from their white brothers and sisters in Christ. History has taught the marginalized to be leery of predators accustomed to devouring them.

Rev. Dr. Mack King Carter, of New Mount Olive Church in Fort Lauderdale, Florida, spoke at the 2012 Samuel DeWitt Proctor Institute where he recounted an episode experienced by his pastor. According to Dr. Carter, when his pastor was a boy walking to school, he would pass a particular house where the white owner would always sic his dog on him. On one particular morning the dog caught the child and bit him. When he arrived at the school his teacher took him to the

---

17. Sarah Kaplan, "For Charleston's Emanuel AME Church, Shooting Is Another Painful Chapter in Rich History," *Washington Post*, June 18, 2015.

doctor and contacted the boy's father, who was a well-known African American Evangelist. As father and son were leaving the doctor's office, the sheriff happened by and asked what happened. The boy's father responded by saying he didn't want to cause problems, but the family of this particular white household would always sic their dog at his boy and today, the dog bit the boy. The sheriff assured the father he would give the family an ultimatum, either build a fence or he would put the dog down. Within two days, a fence surrounded the house. So now, whenever the boy walked by, the dog would rush to the fence barking and growling, trying to get at the boy. According to Dr. Carter, "the dog was constrained but never converted."[18]

Many whites, like the dog, may very well be constrained by laws and regulations, but they have yet to be converted, always looking for a way through, over, or under that fence to devour blacks. For Stacey Floyd-Thomas, the fence will not hold. No permanent fence exists, Floyd-Thomas laments, that will protect us from fenced-in hatred. The will to hate overpowers any obstacle. And because I know she is right, I find myself having to deal with the hopelessness continually created by fenced-in unabated hatred. But as problematic as fences may be, offering forgiveness to the unconverted without building the fence of justice is always deadly to the marginalized. Forgiveness and establishing justice are inseparable parts of the same praxis. True forgiveness, as theologian Juan Luis Segundo reminds us, is only possible if a genuine conversation has occurred. Such a conversation is conscious of the causes of the conflict and has moved to rectify these causes. If not, reconciliation would take place prematurely, masking the existing causes of the conflict and making any just solution impossible to achieve (1993: 37).

Forgiveness devoid of change creates what Adam Clayton Powell Sr. called "cheap grace,"[19] where conversion only occurs in thought and not praxis, leaving in place the underlying causes of oppression. Before forgiveness can be offered, the oppressor must be rebuked and must repent. Any conversation about forgiveness cannot ignore the communal consequences existing beyond the individual(s) offering the forgiveness. Sins of oppression and injustice impact the entire community not just for this generation, but for many generations to come. Roof's

---

18. https://www.youtube.com/watch?v=T8JylbA7ppQ.
19. Dietrich Bonhoeffer, who is usually associated with the term "cheap grace," learned this ethical principle from Powell while attending his church, Abyssinian Baptist Church of Harlem, during Bonhoeffer's student days at Union Theological Seminary.

refusal to repent is in fact a refusal to acknowledge a moral debt. So even if Roof were to repent and beg forgiveness, which he has not, would anyone have the power or right to offer forgiveness and thus redemption for the entire group? To treat Roof's actions as those of a lone wolf, a demented soul, obscures the sociopolitical milieu fostering a history that justifies the societal injustices that gave rise not only to a Roof, but the institutionalization of Roof's prejudices.

True, offering individual forgiveness may lead toward healing for the one victimized. Such forgiveness is offered not for the sake of the powerful or privileged, but for the sake of the one who has been injured. Felicia Sanders, the mother of Tywanza Sanders—Roof's first victim—also attended the Bible study, but survived. During the shooting she shielded her eleven-year-old granddaughter from the assailant. According to Sanders:

> Forgiveness is not for the person. The person doesn't care whether you forgive him or not. Forgiveness is for you. Forgiveness is growth. If you don't have any forgiveness in you, it makes you stagnate. You will never grow. You're giving the individual the power over you, so that means you're still a victim to the person. I want to say that we refuse to be a victim. I want him to know, Prime Evil to know, that just because you took our loved ones, you don't have us. I believe we can get more done now than before.[20]

Forgiveness is first and foremost for healing the oppressed, not absolution for those whose consciences are troubled or burdened with guilt. And while studies show healing can be accelerated if the abused offers forgiveness,[21] in life's messiness, the abused may simply not be ready, requiring more time, even waiting until the next life. Tyrone Sanders, Felicia's husband, is a case in point: "I want to put on the record that I'm not there yet. I don't know if I'll ever forgive." Forgiveness can also be withheld if the injured are made more vulnerable by offering forgiveness (think of an abused spouse).

A distinction exists between the forgiveness offered by an individual and the forgiveness offered by the community-at-large. Offering individual forgiveness as a response to loving one's enemies should not be confused with offering communal forgiveness as a response to estab-

---

20. "Some Forgive, No One Forgets: Charleston, One Year Later," *The New York Times*, June 17, 2016.
21. According to a study conducted by psychologist Robert Enright and psychiatrist Richard Fitzgibbons (2000), which synthesized over twenty years of research, the offer of forgiveness plays a pivotal role in helping those wronged achieve peace of mind and positively deal with their anger so as to relieve depression and anxiety caused by wrongdoings.

lishing justice. These are two different actions occurring at different times. Forgiveness without repentance can occur on the individual level, as offered by some of the victim's family members to Roof. They offer forgiveness as the means by which to restore personal dignity, release resentment, and liberate themselves from the abuser's grip.

But providing communal forgiveness can rob the offender of the opportunity to seriously consider their oppressive acts. Forgiveness offered too soon aborts any opportunity for atonement and repentance on the part of the offenders. Communal forgiveness becomes the decision of the whole not to seek revenge, a decision leading toward and a product of reconciliation. There can be no communal forgiveness without a profound realignment of how power operates within society. While individual forgiveness can be a unilateral act to bring healing to the victim, and possible redemption to the victimizer, communal forgiveness can occur only within a relationship based on justice and equality. Arriving at communal forgiveness is an arduous task, a task that may take several generations to accomplish.

PART III: Sin and Hope as Obstacles to Remembering

The rejection of salvation history in the previous chapters leads to the rejection of total depravity or original sin as a universal theological concept. The fall and depravity of humans are prerequisites for salvation history. Nevertheless, I do agree with Moltmann that inhumanity is more common among us than any positive attributes.

> What true humanity is can be comprehended in a positive affirmation only with extreme difficulty. On the other hand, what inhumanity is—from Nero to Hitler and from the hell of Auschwitz to the hells [in Vietnam] of our own day—can be designated with moderate precision from our experience. (1969: 30)

Regardless of what it might mean to be authentically human, as if we can ever figure out what that means, the empirical evidence points more toward our common inhumanity. Whether inherited or socially constructed, our philosophical discussions fail to provide succor to those crushed by what has become normative. Just because inhumanity is common does not mean the Fall occurred or original sin is a real thing.[22]

22. The theological tenet of original sin does not explicitly appear in the biblical text, although the account of the Fall (Genesis 3) provides tacit substance for speculation. During the Babylonian

Still, the problem with the doctrine of original sin as a stain on one's soul is that it ultimately roots all evil in Adam's original act of disobedience. In short, blaming the original sin of Adam (the Fall) for the sins of oppression prevalent in today's society is a questionable doctrine that obstructs ethical reflection. Most doctrines, either explicitly or implicitly, secure the power and privilege of those formulating the ethical pronouncements of the day. Such doctrines excuse atrocities. After all, we *are* all sinners, and if we *are* all sinners, can any one of us be held accountable? By accepting Jesus all my sins are washed away, cast into the depths of the sea (Mic 7:19)? If my sins are forgotten and forgiven by God, why do I need to dredge them up again?

Moltmann would say, we are humans still in process. "The essence of mankind [*sic*] is hidden and has yet appeared. 'Mankind'—the realized generic concept—is becoming, is still in process, has not yet acquired a fixed 'nature'" (1971: 80). The essence of anything, especially humanity, is problematic for it assumes universalities, which is more a faith statement about some utopian future based on a reality existing neither now, nor in the past—a desire rooted in nothingness. Nevertheless, inhumanity remains a given.

To hope against inhumanity becomes counterproductive for those hoping to survive. Take for example Moltmann's hope for ending oppression: "The crucified Lord embodies the new humanity which responds to God in the circumstances of inhumanity which oppose God. He [*sic*] incorporates home in the circumstances of alienation, and freedom in the midst of chains of slavery. But it is just through this that men are empowered to alter these relationships, to make the world more homelike, and to abolish internal and external slavery" (1974: 116). The answer for humanity is a positive response to the crucified Lord, but unfortunately, it is these same Christians providing a positive response who are responsible for so much hopelessness as they forge

captivity (587–538 BCE), a catalyst for the inception of this doctrine occurred. Hebrew thought was exposed to Persian ideology, specifically the prevalent dualism of good versus evil. The postexilic period saw the emergence of two theories on the fundamental origin of sin. Some linked this origin to an outside diabolic presence (hence Satan as the personification of evil was created) that forced its way into the human condition; others believed sin was naturally inherent. Earlier theologians, e.g. Augustine, emphasized a solidarity with Adam, formulating a doctrine of *peccatum originale*, original sin, graphically depicting humanity's complicity with Adam's rebellion. Augustine grounded original sin in the act of copulation, probably due to his tormented thoughts over his own attitudes toward sex and exacerbated by his sexual urges, as revealed in his classic work *Confessions*. Sin, according to Augustine, was transmitted through "semenal propagation"—the notion that within the father's semen was a generic spiritual substance transferred generationally. This helps explain why a virgin birth was essential to ensure a sinless baby uncontaminated by the earthly father's sin-carrying semen. Every sexual act, even within marriage, became the means by which original sin was transmitted, meaning every sexual act was sinful.

the chains of slavery. No other ideology has brought more enslavement, misery, and death to more of the world's inhabitants than those declaring to be disciples of this crucified Lord. We cannot read Moltmann's faith statement without reminding ourselves of the historical crucifiers who annihilated indigenous people, burned women as witches, conducted inquisitions, led crusades, formed the religious justification for slavery and concentration camps, and established Jim and Jane Crow.

So, as I sat during the first anniversary service of the massacre, I was keenly aware that just a few days earlier, forty-nine mostly young Latinxs were gunned down at the Pulse nightclub in Orlando, Florida. One clear indication of our inhumanity is the devaluation of human life as demonstrated by the US obsession with weapons of mass destruction. Dylann Roof was raised in a culture (God and guns) where he learned that life is cheap and expendable, a culture where he learned some lives matter more than others. The Charleston massacre perpetrated by Roof is but one minor example of our nation's bloodlust.

According to Mass Shooting Tracker, 372 mass shootings[23] occurred in the US in 2015, killing 475 people and wounding 1,870. That's one mass shooting a day! Everytown for Gun Safety tracked sixty-four school shootings in 2015. Gun Violence Achieves documented more than 13,286 people who were killed in the US by firearms in 2015, and 26,819 people who were injured (these figures exclude suicide).[24] For every US soldier killed in Afghanistan during the eleven-year war, thirteen children were killed in the US, for a total of 28,000 during the same time period.[25] No other industrial nation comes close to matching US violence. The number of gun murders per capita in the US in 2012 (the most recent year for comparable statistics) was nearly thirty times that of Britain. Of all the murders that occurred in the US in 2012, 60 percent were by firearms compared with 31 percent in Canada, 18.2 percent in Australia, and just 10 percent in the United Kingdom.[26]

Yes, we are #1 in guns. When compared with the rest of the world, it becomes obvious that there is something fundamentally wrong with our psyche. This doesn't even take into consideration the dispropor-

---

23. A mass shooting is defined as a single shooting incident that kills or injures four or more people, including the assailant.
24. "Guns in the US: The Statistics Behind the Violence," British Broadcasting Corporation, January 5, 2016.
25. Kate Murphy and Jordan Rubio, "At Least 28,000 Children and Teens Were Killed by Guns over an 11-Year Period," *Carnegie-Knight News*, August 16, 2014.
26. "Guns in the US: The Statistics Behind the Violence," British Broadcasting Corporation, January 5, 2016.

tionate number of black lives ended at the hands of the police for minor traffic violations. But it is not just blacks in peril, so are indigenous lives, with almost as many deaths as African Americans at the hands of the police but totally ignored in the conversation. The lives of the undocumented also do not matter, as they find death in the desert because of US immigration laws based on the prevailing *Jaime y Juana Cuervo* policy of deterrence. We are a nation that has made the destruction of bodies of color normative, a praxis legitimized since the first European landed on these shores and killed an Indian who was protecting his or her land from thieves and invaders. And even though life has always been perilous for those with dark skin, because whites have historically devalued the lives of "darker" bodies, they have learned to devalue all lives, regardless of hue, as evident by our gun violence.

The answer to this dilemma for some becomes more guns. According to Charles Cotton, National Rifle Association board member, the shooting at Mother Emanuel was the fault of Pastor Pinckney, who as a legislator voted against carrying concealed handguns in public places. "Innocent people died," according to Cotton, "because of [Pinckney's] position on a political issue."[27] In reality, Roof should never have been able to obtain a firearm after a previous arrest in which he confessed to a narcotics offense. Possessing an illegal substance should disqualify one from obtaining a gun; but the three-day waiting period lapsed due to an administrative error that prevented the FBI from obtaining necessary records. This has come to be known as the "Charleston loophole." The "Charleston loophole" allows gun sellers to continue with the sale if the background check was not completed within the allotted time.

Rev. Sharon Risher, daughter of Ethel Lance who perished during the Bible study, was also planning to be at the one-year memorial service I attended. Instead she was in Washington, DC, sharing her story during a sixteen-hour Democrat-led filibuster demanding stricter gun laws. But while Rev. Risher was in DC advocating gun restriction by connecting our failure to do so with the Charleston and Orlando shootings, Governor Haley and other state Republican elected officials who did appear at the memorial service refused to make the connection of the proliferation of guns with mass shootings. In fact, they never even raised the issue during their presentations, even when South Carolina State Senator Marlon Kimpson (D), who has pushed for a bill for

27. Associated Press, "Charleston Shooting the Fault of Slain Pastor Clementa Pinckney, NRA Board Member Writes," *The Times-Picayune,* June 21, 2015.

expanded background checks, said "we must in Congress and state legislatures address gun reform." Then Governor Haley made her intent clear when she responded, "I don't have anything political to say."

When we consider the connection of gun proliferation to 1) the paranoia, fear, and anti-government sentiments upon which our culture is built, 2) the religious racism upon which our nation was founded, and 3) the support of exceptionalism by nativist politicians to garner votes, we begin to understand that guns serve a *Turner Diaries*-type[28] purpose. The reason for our religious zeal in clinging to our guns is not for hunting or protecting our home—for as Ronald Reagan once observed, you don't need an automatic weapon for either.[29] Such weapons are for rapid and mass killings, to protect from invading armies or zombies. But as neither type of invasion is imminent, our obsession with guns is more likely preparation for a supposedly coming race war in the minds of those who learned the same lessons as Dylann Roof. Open carry applies to one race over against another, and as such, blacks (or Latinxs) cannot safely walk around the city legally carrying an AR-15 as a white man can.[30] Gun rights have not pertained, either now or in the past, to protecting the health and safety of society's nonwhite members.

Creating Tomorrow's History Today

As I sat through the one-year anniversary service, it became clear to me how the narrative of what occurred in Charleston the year before was taking shape. Constructing history occurs early. Certain stories require emphasis; others require silencing. A dominant narrative, as represented by then Governor Nikki Haley (R), is required to mask how racist structures continue to operate in spite of attempts to come together. After the massacre, over twenty thousand held hands across the Arthur Ravenel Bridge. Even Confederate flags came down. Charleston came together in a sign of unity, celebrated by local politi-

28. *The Turner Diaries*, credited as inspiration for the 1995 bombing of the Alfred P. Murrah Federal Building (where FBI offices are located) in Oklahoma City, depicts a violent race war in the United States that leads to the overthrow of the federal government. Jews, gays, and nonwhites are marked for extermination. Excerpts of this white-supremacist novel, which describes the start of a race war with the bombing of F.B.I. headquarters by a homemade truck bomb, were found in the bomber's (Timothy McVeigh's) getaway car.
29. https://www.youtube.com/watch?v=nG4V_6pCLV0, February 6, 1989.
30. http://www.collective-evolution.com/2015/05/18/black-man-vs-white-man-carrying-ar-15-legally-this-is-crazy-video/.

cians as a sign of our humanity. Then Governor Haley (R) saw the good that emerged from the tragedy:

> The good side of it was, I've never been more proud of the people of South Carolina because it should restore everyone's faith in the goodness of people.... People are proud that there weren't protests and negativity. They're proud that the entire state showed what it's like to hold hands together and say we're not going to let hate win.[31]

During the one-year memorial service, the governor spoke of recovery from heartbreak without riots or protests, but vigils instead. Seeking hope in the midst of tragedy is common and understandable. But explaining this tragedy as "God's mysterious ways," as did President Obama during his eulogy, proves problematic for its embrace of a historical Divine plan that excuses evil. "But God works in mysterious ways," said the President. "God had different ideas. [Roof] didn't know he was being used by God."

Although the dominant narrative of hope becomes the foundational interpretation for the future history books to be written, a more critical narrative of the unfolding events may be found on its underside. True—Joseph Darby, presiding elder at the church and first vice-president for the Charleston Branch of the NAACP, believes the shooting could be a catalyst for social change, as the 1963 Birmingham church bombing swayed a nation during the civil rights movement.[32] But before we get too hopeful, it is wise to hear Darby's long critique of all the goodwill following the tragedy:

> We have miles to go to become "post-racial." ... What remains to be seen is whether things have changed in substantial and not symbolic ways. A year has passed since the act of racial terrorism but, in spite of the expressions of goodwill, some things haven't changed. Many of our public schools are still separate and unequal. Racial profiling by law enforcement is still a concern that badly needs illumination. Black families, businesses and churches are still being evicted from the Charleston peninsula through gentrification portrayed as "progress," and lingering social and economic inequities still need to be addressed. The Confederate flag no longer flies at the Statehouse in Columbia, but our governor [Haley] still refuses to accept Medicaid expansion and still opposes rules for reasonable gun control, and our Legislature has yet to pass laws for equity in

---

31. "A Day That Changed Charleston," *The Post and Courier*, June 17, 2016.
32. Debbie Elliott, "While Grieving Continues, Church Shooting Was Charleston's Call to Action," *Morning Edition* on National Public Broadcasting, June 7, 2016.

education and law enforcement. . . . My hope is that the second anniversary of the event will bring more clarity as to whether Charleston has really changed or whether Charleston's response was just the latest in a string of visually appealing but empty and disappointing "Kum By Yah" moments.[33]

Dot Scott expressed her agreement to me: "After a year, no reform has been implemented, so the verdict is still out, the best we can say is it hasn't gotten worse. Distrust between the black community and police is still strong." For Rev. Sharon Risher, daughter of Esther Lance, one of the Emanuel Nine: "The racial tension and history of Charleston is there. It took hundreds of years to build it; it will probably take hundreds of years for people to look at Charleston, South Carolina, as a different place."[34] Holding hands across a bridge may appear hopeful, but history shows it will not lead to institutionalized racism dissipating, politicians placing the needs of the disenfranchised first, or Charleston becoming a postracial city. "Yes, the majority of those on that bridge that day are concerned about racial equality," Ms. Scott told me:

> A desire exists for social engagement as the community participates in joint activities; but seldom do those on the bridge stand up and speak out if there is a cost to them. There is a strong feeling to "move on" without discussing the causes which led up to this particular shooting. At the end of the day, institutional racism remains. But isn't a refusal to discuss the causes which led up to the shooting a type of an abusive relationship?

Maybe the most we can hope for, is confining the dog who refuses to be converted.

In the matrix of numerous remembrances of the tragedy and the consequences for the city that unfolded over the year, how does one find a narrative closer to the truth of what occurred? A preferential historiographical option for narratives emerging from the underside of the official historical account as represented by then Governor Haley, liberationists would argue, is closer to what truly transpired than any history presented from those whose narrative is designed to maintain their power and privilege. True, the Confederate flag did come down from the State Capitol for what appears to be for good. But Rev. Sharon Risher interpreted the act as a political gesture aimed at black people: "Hey, we'll give y'all something all of sudden because one of ours killed

33. "A Day That Changed Charleston," *The Post and Courier*, June 17, 2016.
34. "Some Forgive, No One Forgets: Charleston, One Year Later," *The New York Times*, June 17, 2016.

nine black folks."[35] Removing the Confederate flag, Floyd-Thomas argues, is no different than a Klansman removing his sheet and donning a suit. Nothing changes, except maybe blinding people of color to existing evil, leading some to lower their guard. At least the Confederate flag, like white sheets, eliminates confusion and makes intentions known.

Fueling my sense of hopelessness is the realization that those with sociopolitical power privileges never willingly forsake power unless blood is spilled, all too often the blood of the oppressed. And even then, what is usually offered is symbolism over against substance. A narrative is constructed that serves as an "objective" historical account legitimizing the status quo. Implementing the official historical account breeds hopelessness in those whom this narrative further disenfranchises. But this sense of hopelessness is not despair; rather it is a cold-eyed gaze at the reality of generational oppression and the difficulty for success. Despair leads to giving up. The hopelessness I advocate leads to struggle in spite of the outcome. "How do I give up fighting for justice?" says Dot Scott. "I can't."

The hope offered by Obama during his 2008 presidential campaign ran out during Trump's race-baiting 2016 campaign. No salvation history exists in which Obama is a part of the progressive movement leading America to some postracial future. Since the foundation of what was to become the United States, with the killing of the first Indian and the importing of the first slave, we have been, and continue to be, a racist society, regardless if the emperor was black. There is a certain hubris in this generation, which believes it can eliminate racism because they now see it as wrong. It took over five hundred years to arrive at this point in history; it may take another five hundred years to arrive at a semblance of justice. Or, because history is nonlinear, it could take a season to return to the Jim and Jane Crow attitudes and regulations of the past. Hope in the promised future is supposed to prevent the latter.

During the eulogy of the Emanuel Nine, Reverend Joseph Neal commented: "Senator Pinckney's last act was to open his door to someone he did not know, who did not look like him. So let us not close the doors. Do not let race and politics close the doors that Senator Pinckney opened." The doors of churches, specifically black churches, have

---

35. Sharon Risher, "My Mom Was Killed in the Charleston Shooting. Executing Dylann Roof Won't Bring Her Back," *Vox*, June 15, 2016 (http://www.vox.com/2016/6/15/11894036/dylann-roof-death-penalty).

always been opened for anyone wanting to come and pray, which explains how Roof had such easy access. A year later, the open-door concept seems to have come to an end. As I attempted to conduct my research for this chapter, I found it difficult to enter the church or speak with any minister or member. The gate to the wrought-iron fence surrounding the church was locked. As I attempted to contact the minister, security guards turned me away. In fact, after several attempts, I left Charleston unable to enter Mother Emanuel. Roof's violent acts have left deep scars.

Some of the families of the shooting victims (i.e., Nadine Collier whose mother was killed) no longer attend the church. The needs of the families of the slain have been ignored and the victims overlooked.[36] How does a church bring healing to its members in the midst of visitors all trying to become part of the story? Civil rights activists and sympathizers, mourners of other incidents of gun violence, churches and students, politicians from local to national level, and scholars like myself constantly show up at the church's doors, at times by the busloads. The pastor during the first year after the tragedy, Rev. Betty Deas Clark, wants the doors to remain open to the community and visitors, and she appreciates all the support and love offered by strangers. Still, how can this notoriety be balanced with the need to minister to hurting members if the pews are too crowded for them due to the intense spotlight?[37]

Four days after the massacre, the church reopened its doors for Sunday service. Not all were fine. Polly Sheppard, one of the Bible-study participants who survived the church shooting, thought it was a mistake: "This happened on Wednesday and they were back in church on Sunday, which I thought was terrible." Daniel Simmons Jr., whose father, Rev. Daniel L. Simmons, perished in the attack, agrees. "I don't feel the church should have been opened that soon. Because when I went to the church a couple of days after, I could still sense the smell of blood. . . . It was one of my weakest moments I've experienced throughout this whole process."[38]

I can fully understand the difficulty of entering a once-opened church. To some extent, the church has been turned into a macabre tourist spot as busloads come to witness where the tragedy happened.

36. Andrew Knapp, "For Emanuel AME Church, Nobel Peace Prize Nomination a 'Phenomenal' Honor," *The Post and Courier*, February 1, 2016.
37. Jennifer Berry Hawes, "Journey Through a Year: Emanuel AMC Must Balance National Attention with Ministry to Members," *The Post and Courier*, June 17, 2016.
38. "Some Forgive, No One Forgets: Charleston, One Year Later," *The New York Times*, June 17, 2016.

Joe Darby recognizes that for some, coming to Emanuel is an act of atonement. "There's a need," he says, "particularly for some good white folks to say, 'I am not Dylann Roof. This does not represent me.'"[39] While I understand the need for whites to distance themselves from Roof, I am left wondering if acknowledging racism may prove more healing for whites and the Emanuel Church community.

39. Debbie Elliott, "How a Shooting Changed Charleston's Oldest Black Church," *All Things Considered* on National Public Broadcasting, June 8, 2016.

5

F*ck It

As we observed in the previous chapter, black lives really do not matter to white Christian society. They did not matter when Africans were brought to the Western Hemisphere to work as slaves, and they do not matter today. Whenever the lives of one group do not matter because they fall short of the white ideal, then the lives of all who fall short of the white ideal, who remain outside of history, also fail to matter. Numerous academic studies on the consequences of current US social, political, and economic structures indicate that only white lives continue to matter. While this author has no desire to diminish the work and consciousness-raising conducted by the Black Lives Matter movement, nonetheless, concerns about a neat white/black binary remain problematic.

Even President Obama's simplistic justification as to why black lives matter was troublesome: "I think the reason the organizers used the phrase 'black lives matter' was not because they were suggesting that nobody else's lives matter; rather, what they were suggesting was that there is a specific problem that is happening in the African-American community that is not happening in other communities."[1] What is so worrisome about the president's statement is the lack of awareness about the Latinx social location during his administration, specifically:

---

1. Gardiner Harris, "Obama, in Call for Reform, Defends the Black Lives Matter Movement," *The New York Times*, October 23, 2015.

1) five brown undocumented lives are lost every four days while crossing the desert;[2] 2) second to African Americans, the rate of Latinx killings by police in the first half of 2016 stood at 16 percent of all police killings;[3] 3) Latinxs, who comprised 17.6 percent of the population in 2016, represented 23 percent of all police searches and nearly 30 percent of arrests;[4] 4) thanks to our current immigration laws, Latinxs now comprise the majority of all people in federal prison;[5] 5) the Obama administration (through 2014) has deported over 2.5 million people (23 percent higher than his predecessor George W. Bush), more than any other president, earning him the nickname "Deporter-in-Chief";[6] 6) 25.3 percent of Latinxs live in poverty (compared to 25.8 percent of African Americans);[7] 7) and Latinx have also experienced a US history of lynching throughout the Southwest.[8] These measurable experiences are not an attempt to compare two minoritized communities to figure out who is suffering more. Listing these statistics demonstrates, contrary to the president's pronouncements, that the specific problem occurring within the African American community is also happening in other communities—specifically, for the purposes of this final chapter, the Latinx community.

These specific problems experienced by brown bodies (although not exclusively by them) indicate an invisibility fostered by conservatives and liberals as well as blacks and whites. Not only are whites responsible for participating in the relegation of Latinxs to the invisible underside of history, but so too is the complicity of other communities of color who accept a zero-sum mentality that assumes any advances made by one marginalized group are at the expense of other marginalized communities. This invisibility is what fuels so much of the hopelessness discussed thus far in this book. Not to be seen is a worse fate than simply being dismissed, for at least the one who dismisses must

2. Fernanda Santos and Rebekah Zemansky, "Arizona Desert Swallows Migrants on Riskier Trails," *The New York Times*, May 20, 2013.

3. Kenya Downs, "Why Aren't More People Talking About Latinos Killed by Police?" PBS Newshour: Race Matters, July 14, 2016.

4. Ibid.

5. Solomon Moore, "Study Shows Sharp Rise in Latino Federal Convicts," *The New York Times*, February 18, 2009; and Jennifer Steinhaur, "Bipartisan Push Builds to Relax Sentencing Laws," *The New York Times*, July 28, 2015.

6. United States Department of Homeland Security, *Yearbook of Immigration Statistics: 2013* (Washington, DC: US Department of Homeland Security, Office of Immigration Statistics, 2014), 103.

7. "Quarter of US Hispanics Live in Poverty, Census Says," *Latin American Herald Tribune*, September 1, 2016.

8. Richard Delgado, "The Law of the Noose: A History of Latino Lynching," *Harvard Civil Rights-Civil Liberties Law Review* 44 (2009): 298–302.

first recognize one's being. And yet, when brown bodies are seen, they become the object of fear.

When fear and hatred win, as witnessed in the November 2016 election, violence becomes the new means of communication. We have gone from a political correctness that masked racism and ethnic discrimination to a full-blown demonstration of revenge for years of people of color striving to hold whites accountable in matters of equality, justice, and respect for diversity. Within twenty-four hours of Trump's win, Mark Potok, of the Southern Poverty Law Center, confirmed "seeing a rash of hate crimes, of hate rhetoric, racist graffiti in campuses around the country. We have seen [Ku Klux] Klan literature drops, we have seen that suicide hotlines are ringing off the hook, and we have heard of very extensive bullying in and around schools."[9]

As a Latino, I was not surprised that the candidate who won the 2016 presidency began his campaign calling my people rapists and thieves and promised to respond by building a wall. If every four days, five brown bodies perish in the desert, a wall will only inflate those numbers. The candidate who won made it clear that black lives do not matter, emboldening those for whom they never did matter to applaud a Justice Department led by anti–civil rights individuals like Jeff Sessions. The candidate who won consistently demeaned women's bodies and excused predatory sexual behavior as "locker-room talk," thus heartening a new generation of misogynists. The candidate who won made Islamophobia central to his campaign, raising the specter of future religious-based battles (i.e., travel bans). What the election of Trump successfully accomplished was the ripple effect of a false liberal postracial construct, revealing the true hopelessness faced by marginalized communities.

The invisibility and hopelessness of the migrants' plight is why I walk the trails the undocumented take. For by writing what I see, I can raise the consciousness of my readers. These are unforgiving terrains where daytime temperatures can exceed 115 degrees Fahrenheit (higher during summer months), often leading to death by dehydration. Night-time temperatures can drastically plunge to the point of causing hypothermia. Yes—migrants can freeze to death in the desert! They face the dangers of rattlesnake bites, falling into canyons (making the retrieval of bodies difficult if not impossible), and, due to night-time walking, suffering a misstep that can cause a broken foot or

9. Asher Klein, "'Rash of Hate Crimes' Reported Day After Trump's Election," NBC, November 9, 2016.

sprained ankle—a death sentence as the group moves on, leaving the injured person to fend for themselves. In the midst of this desolate land, surrounded by an army of Border Patrol agents and vigilante groups, we decide to make camp. Reverend John Fife, my conversation partner for this final chapter, is also my guide during my stay in the desert. Not only am I grateful for his guidance and wisdom, I am also grateful for the bottle of Kahlúa he brought, which we share around the campfire to take the edge off the cold night.

Fife is best known for his felony conviction during the 1980s as one of the architects of the Sanctuary Movement.[10] Today, he is one of the leading activists of the organization No More Death, responsible for providing food, water, and medical attention to the undocumented traversing these trails. The camp where we will spend the night has a medical tent that provides life-saving procedures to desperate people. I have witnessed individuals in camp with bloody blisters as big around as baseballs on both feet, unable to walk. As I lay in my sleeping bag during the first night below a breathtaking canopy of stars, I wonder what level of desperation would lead families to risk their lives to cross such a hostile land. Literally, they walk through the valley of the shadow of death.

PART I: Understanding the US Immigration Crisis

In the matrix of different historical perspectives, which ones are closer to understanding the present immigration dilemma? A current immigration crisis exists as the consequence of the ignored, forgotten, silenced, or misinterpreted historical events that benefited white supremacy's past transnational ventures. We (I include myself here as a once-undocumented immigrant) reside in the heart of the empire because we followed our stolen resources and cheap labor. Because the United Stated sent marines throughout the nineteenth and twentieth century to establish roads into our Latinxs' countries of origins, should we truly be surprised when the inhabitants of those countries take those same roads to follow their stolen goods?

Recognizing US-Latin American history as the former's plunder and rape of the lands of the latter is not some alternative leftist interpretation, but acknowledgment of a reality all too often ignored or suppressed. And while the quote may be long, it is worth paying attention

---

10. The Sanctuary Movement was a religious and political campaign to provide safe-haven for Central American refugees fleeing civil conflict in their homelands during the 1980s.

to a voice for justice that arose among Euroamericans. Major General Smedley D. Butler, USMC, who fought for the United States in the Philippines, China, Central America, the Caribbean, and in France during World War I, was the most decorated marine in US history at the time of his death in 1940. He wrote, "War is just a racket":

> A racket is best described, I believe, as something that is not what it seems to the majority of people. Only a small inside group knows what it is about. It is conducted for the benefit of the very few at the expense of the masses.... [Basically] the flag follows the dollar and the soldiers follow the flag.... I spent most of my time being a high-class muscle-man for Big Business, for Wall Street and for the Bankers. In short, I was a racketeer, a gangster for capitalism.... I helped make Mexico, especially Tampico, safe for American oil interests in 1914. I helped make Haiti and Cuba a decent place for the National City Bank boys to collect revenues in. I helped in the raping of half a dozen Central American republics for the benefits of Wall Street. The record of racketeering is long. I helped purify Nicaragua for the international banking house of Brown Brothers in 1909–1912. I brought light to the Dominican Republic for American sugar interests in 1916. In China I helped to see to it that Standard Oil went its way unmolested.... Looking back on it, I feel that I could have given Al Capone a few hints. (Butler 1935)

The most powerful military force the world has ever known, according to the Major General, exists to make sure the majority of the world's resources flow toward the United States. If not for the incursion into Latin America to extract its labor and resources, the US would never have become the global superpower it is today.

The United States has Mexicans crossing the border due to its history of land grab. The "racket" spoken about by Major General Butler is an integral component of ignored and forgotten US history. The same Manifest Destiny ideology explored in the second chapter, which led to the Sand Creek Massacre, explains the current carnage of brown bodies along the southwestern US-Mexican border, sacrificed on the altar of profit-making. For the United States to exist in its present form, not only was it necessary to evict or exterminate the indigenous population, but the territories of sovereign nations to the south required conquest. Manifest Destiny justified the southward crossing of the borders between Texas and northern Mexico, extending US boundaries by physically possessing and repopulating newly conquered and invaded lands. James K. Polk, the eleventh president, was a staunch supporter of Manifest Destiny and promised while on the campaign trail to annex

Texas and engage Mexico in war if elected. Once taking office, he deployed troops in July 1845 under the command of General Zachary Taylor (future twelfth president) into Mexican territory to incite the Mexicans to fire upon the invading US army.

The Mexican-American War ended with Mexico's capitulation and the signing of the 1848 Treaty of Guadalupe-Hidalgo, which ceded half of her territory to the United States. Acquiring the land that became the southwestern United States was more than simply divine inspiration. The new possessions came with gold deposits in California, copper deposits in Arizona and New Mexico, silver deposits in Nevada, oil in Texas, and all of the natural harbors (except Veracruz) necessary for commerce along the California coast. Ignoring the provisions of the peace treaty signed with Mexico allowed the US government to dismiss the historic land titles Mexicans held, sanctioning white US citizens to obtain the natural resources embedded in the land previously held by Mexicans. Mexicans woke up to find themselves now living in the United States, reduced to a "reserve army" of laborers. Thus, the overall southwestern economy developed at their expense. Out of necessity, Mexican Americans worked in the mining and agriculture industry at the lowest wage level, thereby consolidating the power and wealth of the Euroamerican invaders. These natural resources, along with cheap Mexican labor, allowed the overall US economy to develop, expand, and function, while economically dooming Mexico by preventing the nation from capitalizing on its now-stolen natural resources. And here is the irony: it was the invading hordes of whites who conquered the lands of a sovereign nation and constructed the previous inhabitants (many whose roots are indigenous) as illegal immigrants.

While a history of Manifest Destiny helps explain the physical conquest of the land, economic treaties like the North American Free Trade Agreement (NAFTA) explain the economic conquest. Hardest hit by NAFTA's 1994 ratification were rural peasants. Through NAFTA, a concerted shift was made from Mexican food self-sufficiency to reliance on mainly US food imports to free up a land-based workforce to serve as surplus labor at manufacturing plants (known as *maquiladoras* or *maquilas*), most of which are US-owned and -operated (Fitting 2011: 21–22, 103, 109). NAFTA was designed to freely move the goods assembled across borders, free from tariffs or taxes. These maquiladoras allow their US owners (as well as some Mexican and Asian owners) to profit from low wages paid to workers and by the duty charged only on the "value added."[11] In effect, Mexican goods are exported northward, disembodied from the flesh-and-blood Mexicans responsible for the labor and production.

The border fence, while supposedly impenetrable when it comes to the movement of human bodies, remains porous to neoliberalism as US finished goods flow southwards and cheap labor from maquiladoras flows in the opposite direction—unabated. These maquiladoras have become a refuge for former *campesinos* who can no longer compete with subsidized agricultural goods imported from the United States. Unable to achieve financial self-sufficiency through farming, they move northward to the industrial areas along the border to find employment. Even if employment at a *maquila* is obtained, wages earned fall far too short.

In 1975, Mexican production workers were earning 23 percent of US wages. Even with the relocation of US jobs to Mexico, that number dropped to 11 percent. Women fared worse as poverty rates for households headed by women increased by 50 percent (LCLAA 2004: 5). By 2014, the federal minimum wage was 67 Mexican pesos a day ($5.12 US). Since 1976, the last time the federal minimum wage was raised, Mexican wages have lost 71 percent of their purchasing value.[12] The Mexican poverty rate, defined as living on 2,542 pesos ($157.70 US) a month, and as of 2014 stood at 46.2 percent, or about 55.3 of the 120 million inhabitants.[13] Lack of a living wage is but one of the negative impacts NAFTA has had on Mexico, which has one of the lowest minimum wages in the hemisphere. The former *campesino* now working in one of the *maquiladoras* for a few dollars a day looks across the border wall and sees salvation through earning US wages.

The US public creates a narrative that scapegoats Mexican migrants for the current immigration crisis even though NAFTA is the main reason for undocumented migrants' presence in the US, a consequence that immigration experts call the "push-and-pull" factor. The economic conditions created by NAFTA "push" them out, while the US need for cheap labor "pulls" them in. Undocumented presence in the US is not an attempt to force themselves upon an unwilling host country; rather it is the result of global neoliberal economic conditions created, in good measure, by US trade and foreign policies. I walk the migrant trails leaving food and water because our trade policies profit

11. Value added is understood as the value of the finished product minus the total cost of the imported components.
12. Juan Montes, "Mexico Looks to Raise Wages," *The Wall Street Journal*, August 28, 2014.
13. Reuters, "Mexico Poverty Rate Hit 46.2% Last Year as 2 Million More Join Ranks of Poor," *Japan Times*, July 24, 2015.

US businesses at the expense of farmers in two-thirds world nations. When a *campesino* is no longer able to grow his or her crops because of the inability to compete in the marketplace against US subsidized produce, they have little choice but to abandon their lands—the land of their ancestors—and venture into the cities with the hope of finding jobs in one of the *maquiladoras*. When such jobs are insufficient for survival, financial desperation leads many to risk their lives to cross the artificial border.

Rise of an Empire

If the Mexican-American War provided the United States the opportunity to acquire the land of others, then the Spanish-American War provided the opportunity to acquire the economies of others. Prior to the start of the twentieth century, a group of political leaders socializing at the Metropolitan Club in Washington, DC, discussed how the US could become a first-rate nation, despite being saddled with second-rate military machinery. They jealously saw European powers carving up the world for colonial exploitation (Berlin Conference of 1884) and believed the United States must also enter the race to conquer foreign lands. The opportunity presented itself during Cuba's third attempt (1895) for independence from Spain. The late nineteenth century represents a transition in the United States from competitive capitalism toward monopoly capitalism, an economic shift in capitalism that merged with imperialism and found its first expression in the Caribbean and the Philippines. Maturing as an empire, the United States was less interested in acquiring territory than in controlling peripheral economies to obtain financial benefits for the center.

Senator John Mellen Thurston, a former solicitor for the Union Pacific Railroad, bluntly expressed the immediate benefit for challenging the Spanish empire: "War with Spain would increase the business and earnings of every American railroad, it would increase the output of every American factory, it would stimulate every branch of industry and domestic commerce, it would greatly increase the demand for American labor and in the end every certificate that represented a share in any American business enterprise would be worth more money than it is today" (Thomas 1971: 371). Submitting the economies of Spain's former Caribbean colonies to the United States aggravated several major socioeconomic problems: 1) the Caribbean islands developed a slow rate of economic growth due to massive US capital investments that created economic dependency; 2) the cultivation of sugar created classical monoculture colonies where a single crop was produced for export to a single market; 3) the domination of the economy created political dependency on the United States as the islands became part of the US monetary system; 4) the islands suffered from large inequalities in living standards, particularly between the urban and rural populations; and 5) the islands suffered from high rates of unemployment and underemployment. During the 1950s, *el tiempo muerto* (the dead time—May through October when little work in cane fields is required) was particularly devastating, causing rural unemployment and mass migration to the United States.

At the start of the twentieth century, then-President Theodore Roosevelt pursued "gunboat diplomacy" and a policy of "speak[ing] softly but carry[ing] a big stick." These international policies laid the foundation for the development of today's multinational corporations. Roosevelt's foreign policy described how the full force of the US military, specifically the marines, was at the disposal of US corporations, specifically the notorious United Fruit Company, to protect their business interests. Nicknamed "El Pulpo" (the Octopus) because its tentacles extended into every power structure in Central America, the United Fruit Company was able to set prices, taxes, and employee treatment free from local government intervention. Any nation in "our" hemisphere attempting to claim their own sovereignty to the detriment of US business interests could expect the US to invade and/or be victims of a CIA operation with the goal of setting up a new, "friendly" government (hence the term "banana republic"—coined in 1935 to describe servile dictatorships). It is no coincidence that the rise of US banana consumption coincided with US imperialism throughout the Caribbean Basin (Striffler and Moberg 2003: 63, 90, 193, 218).

Throughout the twentieth century, eleven Caribbean countries experienced twenty-one US military invasions and twenty-six covert operations.[14] No country could determine its own destiny without the express permission of the US ambassador to that country. The consequences resulting from US-installed governments—often military

---

14. During the twentieth century, either US military incursions or covert/indirect operations (**bold**) occurred in the following countries so as to bring about regime change or protect the status quo: Cuba, 1906, 1912, 1917, 1933, **1960**, **1961**; Costa Rica, **1948**; Dominican Republic, **1904**, 1916–24, **1930**, **1963**, 1965; El Salvador, **1932**, **1944**, **1960**, **1980**, **1984**; Granada, 1983; Guatemala, **1921**, **1954**, 1960, **1963**, **1966**; Haiti, **1915**, 1994; Honduras, 1905, 1907, **1911**, **1943**, **1980**; Mexico, 1905, 1914, 1917; Nicaragua, **1909**, 1910, 1912, 1926, **1934**, **1981**, **1983**, **1984**; Panama, 1908, 1918, 1925, **1941**, **1981**, 1989.

dictatorships—were massive poverty and inequality, strife, kidnapping, torture, and death. During the 1980s, US foreign policies designed to safeguard established "banana republics" in Central America led to military conflicts in places like El Salvador, Honduras, and Guatemala—the same countries from which most Central Americans migrate to the US. The reason these migrants are on our borders today is directly linked to over a century of US imperialism on their soils.

Whether from Mexico, the Caribbean, or Central America, Latinxs are in the United States not due to some romanticized vision of seeking freedom and opportunity. Nor are they here due to some racist delusion of seeking welfare, free services, and white women. Latinxs are here due to the consequences of past transnational events ignored by official US history. But because any conversation about restitution for US wrongdoings in Latin America would weaken Eurocentric power and privilege, the illusion of a city upon the hill must be maintained.

PART II: Hopelessness as an Impetus for Praxis

The ignored and forgotten US history of incursion into Latinx lands of origin is responsible for today's immigration crises. I would argue that these migrants do not cross borders hoping for a better future, they cross escaping desperate conditions mainly created by US avarice. They cross because staying means death. They cross because there is no other hope. True, I have spoken to some migrants whose crossing success is credited to the apparition of the Virgin Mother, or some angel leading them through the desert while providing hope. And I have no desire to debunk the faith of those motivated by desperation. Still, I am well aware of many of the other faithful whose bodies litter the desert, to whom neither María nor an angel appeared as desert guides. If such manifestation occurred, they were very arbitrary. Still, can something good come to the oppressed who hopes? Sure, why not? Hope might very well work for good as long as it is kept in the realm of the individual. Think of the often told sermon illustration of the child after the storm, walking along the beach making a difference to the one starfish picked up and thrown back into the ocean. The grumpy old man in the parable—who refuses to celebrate the one thrown back into the sea and instead cries for the thousands upon thousands who washed up on the seashore who will perish—has a better grasp of reality. Salvation for starfish, as humans, remains uncomfortably arbitrary.

Where does hope exist for generation after generation of the disenfranchised? When hope is professed by those from the dominant culture, it smacks of egoism that consciously or unconsciously blames victims on the underside of history. According to Moltmann:

> [I]n the promise of God [hope] can see a future also for the transient, the dying and the dead. That is why it can be said that living without hope is like no longer living. Hell is hopelessness, and it is not for nothing that at the entrance to Dante's hell there stand the words: "Abandon hope, all ye who enter here." (1967: 32)

But what Moltmann misses is that while he is correct to observe "Hell is hopelessness," Hell is where the vast majority of the world's oppressed currently live. And the question consistently ignored is: Who benefits from the creation of this Hell?

Those who constructed this Hell, sustain and maintain this Hell, and enjoy the privileges produced by this Hell attempt to provide hope to those living in Hell. It is somewhat disingenuous to tell Hell's occupants they should believe in God's promises for future eschatological possibilities of redemption. Make no mistake, the Hell of crossing the desert is the end product of rapacious US foreign and economic policies in Mexico, the Caribbean, and Central America. How do you prevent desperate people from risking everything in these remote lands and entering the US, people who are highly motivated to find work to feed and clothe the families left behind? You do this by not only making it deadly, but also hellish to enter the United States.

The premise upon which Operation Gatekeeper—our current southwestern border immigration policy—was based was a policy specifically termed "prevention through deterrence." In an August 1, 2001 letter to the US Senate Committee on the Judiciary, Richard M. Stana of the US General Accounting Office wrote that the ultimate goal of Operation Gatekeeper was "to make it so difficult and costly for aliens to attempt illegal entry that fewer individuals would try" (2001: 1). In other words, making migration a living Hell. What Stana meant by making it costly was more than simply a financial expense. Deterrence is also achieved through the loss of life. Some migrants would die traversing dangerous terrain. But this is fine, because their deaths would deter others from attempting the same hazardous crossing.

The death of brown migrant bodies was not some unforeseen consequence of Operation Gatekeeper, but the cornerstone of the policy itself. And while migrants always faced hazards when crossing the border prior to the implementation of Operation Gatekeeper, migrant deaths prior to the ratification of NAFTA remained rare. Ironically, Operation Gatekeeper failed to deter migration;[15] it has, however, succeeded in killing brown people as pointed out earlier in this chapter, with five preventable migrant deaths every four days.

Besides creating the conditions responsible for migrants' death, immigration policy means that those who are caught face physical abuse. One out of every ten migrants reports some sort of physical abuse while in Border Patrol custody, and one in four report verbal abuse (CLAS, 2013: 24). Patrol agents have been known to kidnap and rape the undocumented, including brown girls as young as fourteen years old.[16] Agents have beaten individuals, like Jose Gutiérrez Guzman, into a comatose state.[17] At times, such abuses lead to death. Between 2010 and 2015, it is estimated at least thirty-nine individuals were killed by the Border Patrol. They include Valerie Munique Tachiquin-Alvarado (thirty-two), a mother of five who, in a residential San Diego suburb, suffered fourteen gunshot wounds inflicted by a plainclothes Border Patrol agent.[18] Since 2014, the Border Patrol has been involved in more fatal shootings than perhaps any other US law enforcement agency, developing a reputation for abuse and corruption. On average, between 2005 and 2012, one border agent was arrested each and every day for misconduct.[19]

In an extensive study conducted by No More Deaths, 32,075 incidents of abuse and mistreatment of migrants by law enforcers were documented. According to the report:

> Individuals suffering severe dehydration are deprived of water; people with life-threatening medical conditions are denied treatment; children and adults are beaten during apprehensions and in custody; family members are separated, their belongings confiscated and not returned; many are crammed into cells and subjected to extreme temperatures, deprived of sleep, and threatened with death by Border Patrol agents. (2011: 4)

Based on almost 13,000 interviews with migrants who were in Border

---

15. The presence of undocumented immigrants has substantially increased from about 8.4 million in 2000 to about 11.3 million in 2015. See Katherine McIntire Peters, "Up Against the Wall," *Government Executive*, October 1, 1996 http://www.govexec.com/archdoc/1096/1096s1.htm.
16. Ildefonso Ortiz, "Agent Sexually Assaults Family, Kidnaps Girl, Commits Suicide," *The Brownsville Herald*, March 13, 2014.
17. https://www.youtube.com/watch?v=xomI5NK01gc.
18. https://www.youtube.com/watch?v=6wV_GMUq2aY&list=PLPW0ddSADS1w1ZiM2ep83ExlVQ-JAwN3mn.
19. Garrett M. Graff, "The Green Monster: How the Border Patrol Became America's Most Out-of-Control Law Enforcement Agency," *Politico Magazine* (November/December 2014).

Patrol custody, the study discovered that only 20 percent of people in custody for more than two days received one meal. Children were more likely than adults to be denied water or given insufficient water. Many of those denied water by Border Patrol were already suffering from moderate to severe dehydration at the time they were apprehended. Physical abuse was reported by 10 percent of interviewees, including teens and children. The report concludes:

> It is clear that instances of mistreatment and abuse in Border Patrol custody are not aberrational. Rather, they reflect common practice for an agency that is part of the largest federal law enforcement body in the country. Many of them plainly meet the definition of torture under international law. No undocumented immigrant is safe when in the custody of US enforcement agents. (Ibid.: 5)

When I consider the hellish conditions under which brown bodies are forced to live, I simply lack the luxury or privilege to hopefully wait with Moltmann for God's future promise to materialize. Too many dead and broken bodies obscure my view of the eschaton. Instead, I call for storming the very gates of Hell not at some future time, but now. Moltmann's theology of hope is in effect a theology of optimism based on a God of process derived from trust in a certain biblical interpretation rooted in linear progressive thinking issuing from the Eurocentric modernity project. And while such a hope may be comforting for middle-class Euroamerican Christians, it falls short and sounds hollow for the disenfranchised.

Rather than the prevailing theology of hope, I call for a theology of desperation that leads to hopelessness. I believe the greatest heroes of history, who have moved mountains for the cause of justice, have been those who out of desperation had no choice but to act. Hope is exhausting and tiresome for those residing in the Hell constructed by those complicit with institutional violence. The hopelessness I advocate rejects quick and easy fixes that temporarily soothe the conscience of the privileged but do not offer a more just social structure based on the empowerment of the world's used and abused. The hopelessness I advocate is not disabling; rather, it is a methodology propelling the marginalized toward liberative praxis—even if said praxis might lead to death in the desert.

Ignoring sin, such as depriving those crossing deserts from the fruits of their labor, reveals a certain arrogance in labeling hopelessness as sin while ignoring complicity with social structures responsible for causing the hopelessness. True, despair may lead to defeatism, apathy, and inertia. When I am in despair, I find comfort rolling up into the fetal position and doing nothing but grinding my teeth and weeping. But hopelessness need not be the product of despair. Hopelessness must be understood as desperation, a desperation rooted in the hope denied. When a people are desperate, they will do whatever it takes to change the situation because nothing is left to lose, even if it means crossing a desert. The Latin root for "desperate" suggests a hopelessness that leads to action, at times reckless action, brought about by great urgency and anxiety. It is not hope that propels people to the desert where more often than not death awaits; it is desperation. How many deserts would you cross to feed your children regardless of the risks involved? Hopelessness is an act of courage to embrace reality and to act even when the odds are in favor of defeat. Only at this critical junction of desperation, rooted in the now, is there a possibility for revolutionary change whose consequences might impact the future, or make the future worse as newer forms of oppression manifest themselves. But because we cannot discern the future with any accuracy, and because the future is not determined, we can only and boldly engage in liberative praxis within the now—and *hope* for the best.

Desperation becomes the means by which we work out our liberation, our salvation, in fear and trembling. But this liberation/salvation we work out is not some egocentric project. What is being worked out is how we stand in solidarity with the hopeless struggling for their liberation/salvation. To stand in solidarity with those facing genocide, pauperization, and unmitigated hatred prevents any simplistic platitudes on hope. For hearts to weep and bleed, they require brokenness and realism. To stand in solidarity is to stand in the space of the hopelessness they share. We embrace hopelessness when we embrace the sufferers of the world, and in embracing them, we discover our own humanity and salvation, providing impetus to our praxis, for hopelessness is the precursor to resistance and revolution.

Those on the margins have shown that the hopelessness of having nothing to lose propels toward radical praxis. We must be careful not to define hopelessness as resignation, inertia, and melancholy. For many, hopelessness is the realization that all too often crucifixion is an end. This realization can never be relegated as a sin lest it blame the victims for the violence that befalls them. To embrace hopelessness becomes an attempt to figure out how to believe in the midst of the end. To be hopeless is neither ideological nor depressing, because the inevitable is accepted. To be hopeless is to be emboldened, knowing that a different result is not dependent on us (we are not the Savior).

The call for the hopeless is not despair, but perseverance, even when the end is so near. Hopelessness recognizes night is coming. Darkness may defeat us, may even consume us; nonetheless, the hopeless refuse to go silently into the night. In the desperation of the oncoming abyss, one may desire hope for its avoidance of reality; but hopelessness embraces the reality, recognizing that commitment to liberative principles is what defines our very humanity. With Jesus at Gethsemane, the hopeless drink fully from the cup they desperately pray God would take away (Luke 22:42). We can speculate that on the rim of the void, God makes God's presence felt. But even if God remains deaf-and-dumb, even if we share in Jesus's forsakenness upon the cross, our angst makes our presence felt by God. Maybe this is what Job meant when he cried out: "Though God may slay me, I have no other hope" (13:15). The faith of the hopeless cries out to an absent—or worse, a malicious God—choosing to remain faithful in the midst of desperation.

By contrast, Pope Benedict XVI argues that "hope is the fruit of faith" (1989). But rejecting assured but complicit hope does not indicate the tree of faith is fruitless. This is because the faith of the abandoned who cry out that God has forsaken them is a faith without certitude, the space where unbelievers believe. We believe without the certainty of placing our finger (as did Thomas) into the wounds of the crucified, advancing justice without any certain hope of success. So why do we hold on to faith, if only by our fingertips? We pray and seek God, even when silent, not to serve as our private magician and rescue us from the causes of our hopelessness. We pray and seek the face of God to define ourselves, to participate in communion, to converse with what remains beyond. We pursue a breakthrough of the Messiah in the urgency of the now, a God who claims to be Emmanuel even though we may not feel God is with us. We hound the Divine so we can walk through the valley of the shadow of death, fearing no evil.

Hopelessness embraces lament while hope short-circuits the struggle. As an ideology, hope whitewashes reality, preventing praxis from formulating. As a statement of unfounded belief, hope is an illusion beyond critical examination, serving an important middle-class purpose, providing a quasi-religious contentment in the midst of oppression. All too often, hope becomes an excuse not to deal with the reality of injustice. Engagement in positive and liberative praxis, even when the situation is deemed hopeless, remains possible. We continue the struggle for justice not because we hope we will win in the end; we struggle for justice for the sake of justice, regardless of the outcome. And we certainly do not struggle for justice in anticipation of some heavenly reward. There may or may not be a Heaven. Heck, there may or may not be a God. I'll let the theologians attempt to figure out God's existence. As an ethicist, I am more interested, as indicated throughout this book, in the atrocities committed in the name of God. We struggle for justice because we have no other choice, for the struggle defines our very humanity—or lack thereof.

Moltmann argues that hope brings about praxis: "[W]e become active insofar as we hope," for hopelessness impels ethical praxis (2012: 3). I instead argue that hope, as false consciousness, leads to complacency with the oppressive status quo and breeds apathy. As long as hope exists, I might survive forces geared for my destruction. I just have to keep my head down and my voice muted. *Arbeit macht frei.* The disenfranchised often refuse to resist oppressive structures for the sake of survival or the desire to protect loved ones. As political scientist Jon C. Scott points out:

> A cruel paradox of slavery, for example, is that in the interest of slave mothers, whose overriding wish is to keep their children safe and by their side, to train them in the routines of conformity. Out of love, they undertake to socialize their children to please, or at least not anger, their master and mistresses. (1990: 24)

And while we no longer live under slavocarcy, still, the principle of conformity to survive is a reality attested by the working poor within communities of color who learn to keep their mouths shut and avoid political actions lest they find themselves without the means to feed their families.

To hope is to become dependent on the metaphysical to lead toward some utopian future without our need to participate to make the determined future a reality. Looking to occupy the future dictates how I must act in the present. The hope of survival means I have something in the future to lose, and protecting the little I imagine I have blocks me from the radical actions required if drastic change is desired. Those who recognize they have no future are already among the walking dead; but salvation and liberation may be possible by toppling Panopticon. We engage in liberative praxis because there is no choice but to fight for liberation from injustices, a fight for survival. I, of course, am not alone in calling for hopelessness in order to move closer to justice.

Cultural theorist Claire Colebrook, speaking about feminists' struggle for justice, also calls for the abandonment of hope:

> Utopia could only be achieved through an intense hopelessness. Certainly, one of the laments of a perceived post-feminism is that now that women have achieved certain material benefits, there is no longer a desire for radical difference; with some degree of hope, we lose a genuinely feminist future, a future that would seem to be possible as a Utopia only if we could abandon or cease to be fed by these meagre hopes that diminish our force. (2011: 16)

I argue that her analysis is not limited to feminists but to all who are oppressed. Hope prevents all of us from committing to praxis capable of new constructs of reality along with utopian concepts of justice.

Refusing to Romanticize the Hopeless

Reading this book might lead the reader to the wrong conclusion that I am setting up a neat dichotomy: all that is bad is white and all that is good is of color. To make a preferential historiographical option for the narratives of the oppressed does not mean the marginalized are holier, more moral, or saintlier. The oppressed, like oppressors, can also become intoxicated with power and privilege given the oppor-tunity. While in Santiago, Chile, I visited *el museo de la memoria y los derechos humanos* (Museum of Memory and Human Rights), which cata-logues the horrors of torture, disappearance, and murder of thousands of Chileans during the US-backed seventeen-year Pinochet regime. Facing the Wall of Disappeared Persons, one looks into the faces of thousands who simply ceased to exist. Among the more moving item in the museum was the *parrilla*, the Spanish word for barbecue or grill. The victim was stripped naked and strapped (spread-eagle) on his back to a metallic bed-frame. Although the bed was usually hooked up to a standard wall socket, the one on display was attached to a car battery. Either a fixed wire was wrapped around the man's penis or a wire mesh bag was tightly fitted around his genitals. Additionally, a thin metal rod was inserted in his urethra. Women, after being raped, had a metal rod inserted into their vagina, and/or a metal clamp attached to their nip-ples, clitoris, or labia. Like a slab of meat on a grill, the victim was then "cooked."

In La Habana, Cuba, in the *antiguo Palacio Presidencial* (old Presidential Palace) that now serves as *el museo de la Revolución* (the Museum of the

Revolution), are exhibited different instruments of torture used during the US-backed Batista regime. I was drawn to a denailing clipper, a medieval device still favored by autocratic regimes. The metallic contraption looked something like a splint used to set a broken bone; however, at the end of this splint-type gadget, coming over and above the fingertip was an apparatus appearing to be a miniature set of pliers that gently attached to the victim's fingernail. With a firm tug on the splint, the entire fingernail was quickly and efficiently removed. At times the nail would crack and only a portion was removed; but it really didn't matter—the results were the same—excruciating pain.

Care should be taken not to conclude that inhuman treatment is exclusively characteristic of conservative, right-leaning regimes like the US-backed Pinochet or Batista governments. The political turnover of prison officials at the nondescript neo-Renaissance building located on Andrássy Boulevard 60 in Budapest, Hungary or the Seodaemun Prison in Seoul, Korea indicates how inhumanity is not limited to one particular political leaning or ideology. Known as the *Hüség Háza* (House of Loyalty) in Budapest, the building served as the party headquarters of Hungarian Nazis (the Arrow Cross Party) between 1944 and 1945. As the Soviet tanks entered the city to push out the Nazis, one of their first acts was to take over this building. The leftist victims of the Nazis became the new oppressors, using the same gruesome torture techniques, from 1946 until 1956. The building became the new headquarters for the *Magyar Államrendőrség Államvédelmi Osztálya* (Hungarian State Police State Protection Department) or ÁVO, succeeded by the *Államvédelmi Hatóság* (State Protection Authority) or ÁVH, the infernal appendages of the Soviet Union's KGB secret police.

Like the fascists before them, the new communist regime tortured and killed their opponents (or those likely to become dissidents) in its cellars. I visited the basement dungeons where the interrogation and torture occurred. One room was padded. Another was only about five square feet and used for solitary confinement, making lying down almost impossible. In one cell, water was constantly on the floor to prevent a prisoner from ever being dry; in another, electric shocks. One room simply had clubs along the wall—I needed no explanation. And of course, there was an execution room where a noose hung from the ceiling. Both the Right and the Left sent political prisoners to concentration camps. As in the Chilean museum, I was haunted by the Wall of Photos of Political Prisoners, pictures of those who were dragged into this building to be tortured, and in many cases, murdered or disappeared.

Like the *Hüség Háza*, Seodaemun Prison in Seoul, Korea also reveals that brutality exists on both sides of the ideological divide, in this case, among colonizers and colonized. Built in 1908 during the Japanese colonial era, it was designed to imprison five hundred liberationist activists, only to be expanded thirty-fold during the 1930s to provide more space for some 23,500 dissidents. After 1945, with the end of colonial rule, the Japanese overlords were themselves imprisoned in these buildings. During the military regimes from the 1960s through the 1980s, the prison was used by South Koreans to incarcerate and torture pro-democracy South Koreans, thus linking the atrocities that occurred under both colonial and independent South Korea. The prison remained active until 1987, becoming a museum in 1992.

As in Budapest, over a hundred different torture methods were conducted in the basements, where the cells were located. Descending to the basement, I noticed one cell was a temporary holding room where prisoners could hear their compatriots being tortured in the adjacent room. Prisoners were at times placed into vertical claustrophobic coffin boxes to be entombed for long spans of time where any type of movement was impossible. Another small box contained spikes that gently impaled the occupants if they moved an inch in any direction. One cell displayed a mannequin hung upside down as water was poured over its face. Another displayed how sharpened sticks were jabbed under fingernails. A separate building housed the gallows, with a secret tunnel to dispose of the corpse so as to conceal the killings. As in Chile and Hungary, I was most moved by a room bearing some 5,000 portraits of those who died during detention.

Torturers are not limited to authoritarian regimes. Within the United States, in our holy war against terrorism, we engage in our own terrorist acts, even though then-president George W. Bush assured us that "[t]his government does not torture people. We stick to US laws and our international obligations."[20] And yet, even as the president reassured the nation that we were above torture, prisoners were hung up in chains; were placed in stress positions for up to twenty-four hours; were left to urinate or defecate on themselves; were sexually abused by female interrogators; were given forced enemas; were locked into coffin-like boxes; were sleep deprived; were sensory over-

20. https://www.youtube.com/watch?v=g6LtL9lCTRA.

loaded; were subjected to lit cigarettes placed in their ears; were menaced with dogs; were beaten; were waterboarded; were slammed against walls; were subjected to twenty-four hours of nonstop loud music; were choked; were forced into long periods of isolation; were forced to be nude; were subjected to sexual taunts; were subjected to aggressive body cavity searches; were kept in diapers; were used as human mops; were threatened with rape, were subjected to mock executions; were threatened with sexual and physical violence against family members.[21]

In 2004, the American Red Cross charged the United States military with intentionally using psychological and physical coercion tantamount to torture at the Guantánamo Bay detention camp (Gitmo).[22] In 2006, Amnesty International accused the United States of committing widespread abuses, including torture and the continued detention of thousands of individuals without a trial, calling Gitmo "the gulag of our times."[23] As poorly as prisoners are treated at Gitmo, Kenneth Roth, executive director of Human Rights Watch, noted that some were sent to CIA "black sites" while others were handed over to countries like Egypt, Saudi Arabia, and Jordan, that were not averse to employing extreme forms of physical torture to gain information later passed along to the US.[24] Not surprisingly, fifteen years after being freed, former prisoners—according to previously undisclosed medical records, US government documents, and interviews with said prisoners and military and civilian doctors—revealed that many developed persistent mental health problems. Many suffer similar symptoms as former US prisoners-of-war who faced inhumane and cruel treatment decades earlier by some of the world's most brutal regimes.[25] One of those former prisoners, Ahmed Errachidi of Morocco, probably said it best: "It is very, very scary when you are tortured by someone who doesn't believe in torture. You lose faith in everything."[26] I am left wondering

21. Neil A. Lewis and David Johnston, "New FBI Memos Describe Abuses of Iraq Inmates," *The New York Times*, December 21, 2004; "Ex-GI Writes About Interrogation Tactics," *The New York Times*, January 29, 2005; Neil A. Lewis and Eric Schmitt, "Inquiry Finds Abuses at Guantánamo Bay," *The New York Times*, May 1, 2005; Neil A. Lewis, "Fresh Details Emerge on Harsh Methods at Guantánamo," *The New York Times*, January 1, 2005; Matt Apuzzo, Sheri Fink, and James Risen, "US Torture Leaves a Legacy of Detainees with Damaged Minds," *The New York Times*, October 9, 2016.

22. Neil A. Lewis, "Red Cross Finds Detainee Abuse in Guantánamo," *The New York Times*, November 30, 2004.

23. Amnesty International, "Iraq: Beyond Abu Ghraib: Detention and Torture in Iraq" (March 6, 2006): 1–8; Alan Cowell, "US 'Thumbs Its Nose' at Rights, Amnesty Says," *The New York Times*, May 26, 2005.

24. Peter Maass, "Torture, Tough or Lite," *The New York Times*, March 9, 2003.

25. Matt Apuzzo, Sheri Fink, and James Risen, "US Torture Leaves a Legacy of Detainees with Damaged Minds," *The New York Times*, October 9, 2016.

if one day, in some near future, if the portraits of Gitmo's prisoners will hang from the military base walls as a witness, as they do now in Chile, Hungary, and South Korea.

While those accustomed to institutionalized violence can easily detect who are the beneficiaries of the oppressive social structures perpetrated against them, at times they remain oblivious to their own complicity with oppression. Even among colonized communities, structures of intra-oppression flourish. And while the oppressive structures of the dominant culture should never be minimized, it is also important to be aware of the ways the marginalized emulate the dominant culture. Inhumanity is not limited solely to Euroamericans. The danger of any decolonization process is the replication of new oppressive structures where the faces and/or ethnicity of the new oppressors are the same as those who remain disenfranchised. All too often, those more likely to be privileged by internal oppressive structures are those who have experienced colonization but now occupy positions of power. The marginalized often shape themselves in the image of the dominant culture, learning to mimic the attitudes, beliefs, behaviors, and actions they have been taught to see as superior.

Colonized minds reinforce the marginalized lack of self-worth, which often leads to self-loathing. Some marginalized persons seem to attempt assimilation, becoming "whiter" than the dominant culture. If salvation requires assimilation—at least in terms of the dominant culture—then proof of worthiness lies in being accepted by the dominant culture, even if this leads to actions contrary or damning to one's own indigenous community. The lure of becoming new oppressors at the expense of other marginalized groups is a reality finding expression in various forms of oppression within marginalized communities, such as internal racism, sexism, heterosexism, and classism, where proximity to the white heterosexual male ideal remains the standard for measuring superiority. The closer one is to the white ideal (either in physical attributes or geographical proximity), the more privilege—although still limited within the overall dominant culture—exists.

Some within marginalized communities attain "the American dream," or believe they have, proving good things can come to those who hope. Class privilege does create opportunities for some within marginalized groups to participate and benefit from the existing power structures. But to belong can lead to greater disdain and less patience

26. Ibid.

or compassion than their white counterparts for those within their own communities who fall short of the white ideal, usually persons who are darker and poorer. This is evidenced by the number of Latinxs who support anti-immigrant policies and politicians. When the marginalized who vocally support manifestations of white supremacy are lifted onto pedestals, the message to racial and ethnic communities is clear: if you too want to succeed, then emulate these hopeful success stories. The lure of economic privilege has a way of seducing everyone, including those within marginalized groups, to seek benefits for self instead of justice for all.

Alice Walker questioned this phenomenon, lamenting some of the consequences brought about by the civil rights movement: "I think Medgar Evers and Martin Luther King, Jr. would be dismayed by the lack of radicalism in the new black middle class, and discouraged to know that a majority of the black people helped by the Movement of the sixties has abandoned itself to the pursuit of cars, expensive furniture, large houses, and the finest Scotch" (1984: 168). The "pursuit of cars, expensive furniture, large houses, and the finest Scotch" contributes to the rhetoric of hope needed to justify the colorblind "official" history of the dominant culture. Apologists for prevailing injustices are needed, facilitating the offerings of lucrative rewards to such spokespersons.

Assimilation is not the only threat. While some within marginalized communities find salvation through assimilation (a difficult action to unpack because individual motives are always complex), others define liberation by surmounting power structures without dismantling them. Replacing a white dominant culture with a darker hue is not liberation. As Jacques Mallet du Pan reminds us with his 1793 adage, "The Revolution devours its children." The gravest danger arises in the refusal to seriously consider how power works within marginalized communities, which is the danger of emulating oppressors. As Paulo Freire warned, the oppressed almost always, during the initial stage of their struggle, tend themselves to become oppressors (what he called "sub-oppressors") rather than strive for liberation (1968: 27). The very thought process of the oppressed group is shaped and constructed by the oppressive context in which they find themselves. Liberation runs the risk of being defined in Euroamerican terms, usually as equality with the oppressor. In seeking equality, the disenfranchised model themselves in the image of existing power structures designed to privilege one group over another. Liberation is reduced to surmounting

148

present power structures rather than dismantling them so as to reconstruct a more just social system.

That the present power structures are designed to privilege the dominant Euroamerican culture is not questioned. Still, to attack the dominant culture solely for its complicity with the present power structures masks how existing intra-structures of oppression operate. We achieve a new level of maturity when we move beyond what Edward Said terms "the rhetoric of blame," which is to solely attack the dominant culture for being "white, privileged, insensitive, and complicit" (1994: 96). Historically, it has always been easier to blame the dominant culture's oppression, yet all woes faced by the marginalized cannot be solely attributed to Euroamericans. Subscribing to some disenfranchised nativism is to accept the consequences of Eurocentric racism and colonialism, which reinforces subservience, even while attempting to reevaluate the oppressed ethos. Regardless of any aggressive stance taken, the former oppressors are in danger of becoming trapped in a defensive role. Recognizing our own structures of power, which can also oppress, does not minimize the repression imposed by the dominant culture. Rather, it places the focus upon the structures instead of an ethnic group—which in this day and time just happens to be Euroamerican.

PART III: Toward an Ethics para Joder

The process of liberation can lead to new oppressive structures where the formerly oppressed become the new oppressor. Is it any wonder why I argue that all is hopeless? Justice is but a platitude, liberation an impossibility, salvation denied. The issue facing us is how we should ethically respond in the face of hopelessness. We can turn to escapism, which can be manifested in different ways. For some, it may be substance abuse. For others, it might be a deliberating despair. And yet for others, it might be an irrational acceptance of some hopeful future utopia. A more positive approach to hopelessness may be a "f*ck it" praxis that might lead to surviving the chaos and madness of the moment. I have, in previous works, referred to this praxis as an *ethics para joder*. In the preface to this book, titled "The Order of Things," I argued for a liberationist paradigm beginning with praxis, which then leads to doxy. In the first book of the trilogy of which this book is the last, I proposed the ethical praxis *jodiendo*. This entire book was an attempt to create doxy based on the implementation of this praxis. Those familiar with my earlier work may find the final section of this chapter somewhat repetitive; nevertheless, this final book of the trilogy would be incomplete if I failed to end where I began, with praxis—thus closing the hermeneutical circle.

The focus of this book has been history, an ideologically based construct designed to normalize and legitimize the prevailing sociopolitical power structures, making resistance futile. Before the enormity of the white supremacy that undergirds a neoconservatism aiming to globally center whiteness; and before the neoliberal global economic octopus (along with the greatest military power ever known) designed to ensure that the vast majority of the world's resources flow to a Eurocentric minority, dismantling these eco-political structures is truly hopeless. Attempts to do so often end by replacing one elite group with another, leaving the structures intact. Radical change within the lifetimes of the oppressed is limited, providing few ethical alternatives. Liberals and progressives within the dominant culture may have the best of intentions, and may very well participate in paternalistic praxis to save and rescue unfortunate souls; nevertheless, the devastating consequences of neoconservatism and neoliberalism will continue to worsen as the global few get wealthier at the expense of the world's wretched. While conservatives may ignore the plight of the oppressed altogether, offering guilt-relieving charity, liberals might put on a better show of standing in solidarity. Still, few liberals are willing or able to actively dismantle the very global structures designed to privilege them at the expense of the majority of the world's inhabitants (De La Torre 2010: 92).

With hopelessness as a given, the question before us is how to ethically engage in praxis. *Joder* is Spanish for "f*ck it." A politer translation is "to screw with"—not "to screw," but to "screw with," a crucial difference in semantics. Coining a term to describe an ethical practice already occurring among the marginalized implies that this methodology of *jodiendo* already exists. As an organic intellectual, I am simply reflecting upon this existing praxis for the purpose of theorizing and theologizing. An *ethics para joder* is an ethics that f*cks with the prevailing power structures. An *ethics para joder* fosters an effective response to the consequences of Eurocentric globalization, the oppressive normativity of social structures, and the pain of the domestication of communities of color.

A *joderon* is one who strategically becomes a royal pain in the ass, purposely causes trouble, constantly disrupts the established norm, shouts from the mountaintop what is supposed to be kept silent, and audaciously refuses to stay in his or her assigned place. To *joder* is to create instability, upsetting the prevailing Panopticon social order designed to maintain the law and order of the privileged. Instability could lead some within the dominant culture to share in the hopelessness of overcoming the global neoconservative and neoliberal forces, creating an opportunity for change. Yes, a liberative ethics *para joder* is frightening to those accustomed to their power and privilege, because hopelessness signals lack of control. Because those who benefit from the present social structures insist on control, sharing the plight of being vulnerable to forces beyond control will demonstrate how hope falls short (ibid.: 94).

To *joder* refuses to play by the rules established by those who provide a space for orderly dissent that pacifies the need to vent for the marginalized but is designed not to change the power relationships within the existing social structures. Think of Jesus cleansing the Temple, the liberative praxis of literally overturning the established bankers' tables of order and oppression (Matt 21:12–13). To *joder* is to overturn traditional tables. *Joderones* provide a moral justification for the employment of deception as a means of self-preservation for those who face overwhelming odds against surviving. Political and social change requires going beyond the rules created by the dominant culture, moving beyond what is expected, pushing beyond universalized experiences.

History demonstrates the futility of simply denouncing unjust social structures. Those whom the structures privilege will never willingly abdicate what they consider to be their birthright. The *joderon* as trickster creates opportunities unavailable as long as established tables remain stable. F*cking with oppressive structures that undergird exceptionalism might lead to new possibilities. If the prevailing history that justifies the dominant social order, as argued throughout this book, exists to legitimize and normalize the privileges of the few at the expense of many, then *joderones* become tricksters who lie to reveal truth. They lie, cheat, joke, and deceive to unmask deeper truths obscured by the dominant culture's moralists. Such liberative praxis may be dismissed as immoral by the dominant culture; still, tricksters remain ethical, operating in a realm beyond good and evil, beyond what society defines as right or wrong. *Joderones* are consummate survivors, serving as exemplars for the disenfranchised in need of surviving the reality of disenfranchisement. Disrupting the equilibrium of the

151

dominant culture creates compromising situations for those in power, revealing their weaknesses, exposing what they prefer to remain hidden, and removing their artificial masks of superiority.

Current US immigration policies are based upon centuries of racism and ethnic discrimination, starting with the Chinese Exclusion Act of 1882. This is an immigration structure which, among many abuses, includes: 1) the murder of the undocumented in the US, and Mexican nationals while physically in Mexico (De La Torre 2016: 5–7, 37); 2) the physical abuse of the undocumented when apprehended (ibid.: 36–37) and imprisoned (ibid.: 134–38); 3) a kangaroo trial procedure designed to prevent reentry (ibid.: 95–101); 4) and a deportation procedure that steals their meager possessions and separates families, both within the US and once in Mexico (ibid.: 140–41). To believe these oppressive structures can be overturned anytime soon (especially in an era of "build the wall") ignores how entrenched are anti-Latinx sentiments.

An *ethics para joder* is a liberative praxis by which we learn to transform society for the better, even though the ultimate utopian goal may never be realized. Nonetheless, we strive forward not because we hope to succeed (because we won't) or because we cling to a biblical belief that a promise was offered; we move toward justice because we have no other choice if we wish to define ourselves as humans. We strive forward because in the crucible of struggle, we construct our identity and define our purpose in life. And even if you still want to insist on the existence of some utopian hope, then maybe, just maybe, it may be found only when one takes a stand and says "f*ck it."

Faced with the insurmountable task of creating justice-based immigration policies in our lifetime makes f*cking with the immigration system the only ethical response to the immigration dilemma in the *hope* of creating new opportunities through disorder and chaos. In 2012, I was invited to Tucson to present the concept of *an ethics para joder* to several of the humanitarian groups working on the border. Useful to some was a conversation moving away from repeating past praxis simply because these were the liberative actions always undertaken. *Ethics para joder*, according to Fife who attended the discussion, "freed us to imagine new possibilities." I asked him to provide a concrete example. For decades, he explained, they have been fighting for justice, and most have lost hope in succeeding. Many resonated with the explanation about the oppressiveness of hope. When they tried to develop praxis, some were trapped with having to construct actions leading to a specific end goal.

When they accepted the hopelessness of the situation, they were emboldened to simply f*ck with the system, subverting the prevailing oppressive structures. "Screwing with structures of oppression is our calling," said Fife. "We engage in *jodiendo* as we prepare and wait for the movement for justice to take off. Hopelessness frees us to imagine creative ways to struggle for this justice." It is important to note that I did not create a new praxis methodology, I simply named what the marginalized have always done in order to survive. I facilitated an approach for those standing in solidarity with the oppressed to move beyond the piety and moral principles established by those privileged by the ethics of the dominant culture.

This *ethics para joder* was manifested when a dozen activists, on October 11, 2013, chained themselves to the wheels of two prison transport buses carrying the undocumented to trial (ibid.: 103–4). It may be hopeless to think a few activist organizations will defeat the private prisons like Correction Corporation of America and the GEO Group, along with the many politicians they finance to uphold the prison-industrial complex. And yet, such negative publicity has the potential to raise consciousness.

On December 14, 2015, eight clergy members, including Fife, disrupted an Operation Streamline court hearing when ministers stood up, one-by-one, and offered prayers or read Scripture, disrupting the so-called "legal" procedures. "I stood in Streamline court today and spoke," Fife said, "because I have watched too long in silence as Streamline has violated human rights, the constitution, legal ethics, and my faith. I was called to speak this truth to those responsible, and to bless the poor." In a joint written statement explaining their actions, the participating clergy stated:

> We have disrupted the courts and we do not do so lightly, for the courtroom is in its own way a sacred place. But we disrupted the proceedings today because they have already been disrupted in a much more troubling way by Operation Streamline. It is clear to us that Operation Streamline is immoral, unjust, and a sin against the poor and their families, and as pastors in this community we have an obligation to speak. And so our witness in the court and in the public square today is: "You [the shackled migrant workers] are not guilty—this court is guilty of injustice to the migrant poor and their families. *¡Tu no eres culpable, este corte es culpable!*" (ibid.: 106–7)

To *joder* is not a praxis in which disenfranchised groups engage out of a desire for vengeance. To *joder* is an act of love toward oppressors, designed to force them to live up to their rhetoric in the hopes of confronting their complicity with oppressive structures so as to lead them toward their own salvation. Oppressors are also victims of structures designed to privilege them yet rob them of what it means to be human. To *joder* is thus far a nonviolent survival strategy based on love designed to liberate the abused from death-dealing social structures that deny their humanity, and the abusers whose own humanity is lost through their complicity with these same structures.

Please, Please, End on a Note of Hope

You have faithfully read this entire book and have finally arrived at the final pages. Here is where I am supposed to tie a red ribbon around this project and provide clear, neat conclusions. If readers were looking for answers, then I fear they might leave with questions; if they were looking for certainties, they will leave with contradictions; if they were looking for order to their lives, they will find a messier existence. And if they were looking for hope, they surely will leave with a deeper sense of desperation. I confess at times while typing the words for these concepts and thoughts, I felt the pull toward providing a happy ending, a resolution to the human dilemma I explored, to joyfully sing "It is well with my soul." Oh, how much more comforting it would be to proclaim in these final pages "God is good—always!" With all my heart, soul, mind, and body, I wish to become intoxicated with the simplicity of unquestionable and uncomplicated faith. But to do so would be an insult to the vast majority of humanity scraping by at the margins of society, and an insult to an absent God in whom I grudgingly choose to believe, regardless of whether said God exists.

Fortunately, my God neither trembles nor frets over my cross-examinations. Could this be the ultimate beauty of faith—to doubt, to curse, to wrestle, to disbelieve, to think? Relying on hope due to some faith-based ideology, regardless of how tempting it might be, is but an illusion resting on the mirage of a teleological eschatology based solely on an unflinching desire that it be so. By now, the reader realizes that my call in embracing hopelessness is not a cynical admission, leading many to throw their hands up to the sky and cry "Why bother?" Such a response to reality is a middle-class privilege unaffordable to the marginalized who must continue to struggle if they wish to survive. Besides, it is hope that cuts short the career of many social workers who pursue a life of making a difference because they believe they can actually make a difference—a type of messiah complex. How much healthier to admit that none of us are Saviors, and instead struggle for justice knowing the battle is already lost and history stands against us.

For those who occupy spaces within the dominant culture, please refuse the temptation to insist the oppressed must have hope. Those living with privilege see as normative a life full of hope for the future. But hope cannot be imposed. If the disenfranchised dared to share the hopelessness of their situations, those with privilege might realize their charitable works are simply insufficient. Perhaps the answer will never be charity but rather restructuring power structures. I conclude this book embracing hopelessness, believing it to be more productive if we don't rely so heavily on hope, specifically the hope of the dominant culture, which serves as a tyranny preventing praxis and preserving privilege. When hope becomes an antidote for the guilt of the privileged, eliciting *mea culpas* and profound apologies, it carries with it a refusal to tamper with the self-perpetuating structures responsible for creating and reinforcing injustice. The semblance of hope becomes an obstacle when it serves as a mechanism to maintain, rather than challenge, the prevailing social structures.

The hope offered by the dominant culture appears too contrived, too forced. Such temporal hope holds little sway in the world of the exploited. To be blunt, I hold little, if any hope for justice in my time. Working for justice, liberation, and salvation, as already mentioned, is not conducted because there is hope of success. The disenfranchised undertake this work because no other alternative exists. Even in the absence of any assurance of future success, the work toward justice continues for its own sake.

To be hopeless is a desperation refusing to give up, a recognition that even if carrying the cross leads to crucifixion, the struggle for justice is what defines the present and could plant seeds that might blossom in some future. Fruit might someday be borne, but that is inconsequential for those suffering in the now. And while there is nothing redemptive in the present suffering, nevertheless, it marks a refusal of complicity with the inhumanity undergirding oppression. Yes, we should do everything in our power to avoid decimation and destruction. Martyrdom is not something to be sought; but at times death cannot be avoided, for it provides meaning and purpose to life. As my intellectual mentor would say: *Moriré de cara al sol.* Justice probably will not be the determined future of humanity; nevertheless, its pursuit is what makes life worth living in the present—and maybe, just maybe, this is what it means to hope against all hope.

6

Poetic Epilogue

¡Esperando esperanza
no es para los pobres
los jodidos debe aprender
a joder a los joderones!

For those lacking dexterity to sing in two cultures
ignorant of the language of angels
and sung by radical revolutionaries
allow me to translate these vulgar verses.

Waiting for hope
is not for the poor
those who are screwed must learn
how to screw with the screwers!

What's vulgar are not these simple verses
for vulgarities are personal pieties
imposed on chosen words
rather than the dispossessed miseries.

I am hopeless
before structural subjugation

silk sandals exchanged for the homeless
the air in their lungs ripe for capitalization.

I am hopeless
before structural subjugation
where the wretched lack wholeness
yet fight for their liberation.

So do not peddle this hope opiate
ignoring middle-class power
do not sell me this hope tonic
as I am marched to the gas showers.

So do not preach this hope theorem
where from trees swing strange fruit
do not prescribe this hope serum
while discarded refuse litter deserts.

Let their forgotten stories reverberate through your being.
Let their silent voices course through your veins.
Let their convictions tug at your heart.
Let their sufferings gnaw at your brain.

Become lanterns illuminating the dispossessed
bringing to light the plight of the transgressed
revealing the persecution of the repressed
shining a beam on the repression of the oppressed.

Stand committed to solidarity with the hopeless.
Stand rebelling against the neoliberalism that subjugates.
Stand proclaiming the good news of liberation to the helpless.
Stand subverting the social structures that segregate.

Be not a Christian soldier marching as to war
be not a crusader crushing infidels for Christ
but be lambs before the slaughter
gentle doves before the wolves.

In solidarity with the hopeless
stand disruptive yet decisive

feeling desperation not despair
agitating not assimilating.

So do not be tempted with riches of some afterlife.
Spare me from pious pontifications of future rewards.
Insult me not with Roman's road to salvation.
Convince me instead by sacrificial agape here and now.

So offer not your words of hope.
Offer your praxis for justice.
Shower me not with God's future promises.
Show God's present grace though your loving mercy.

So when hawkers of hope seduce you to join them
and when rationalists wonder why you struggle for justice's
    unwinnable odds
and when charlatans peddle revelation as revolution
and when a world gone mad questions your very sanity
you can respond in confidence and boldness
I am hopeless.

Bibliography

Adorno, Theodor. *Minima Moralia: Reflections from Damaged Life*. Translated by E. F. N. Jephcott. London: Verso, 1997 [1951].

Ahlstrom, Sydney E. *A Religious History of the American People*. New Haven: Yale University Press, 1972.

Aquino, María Pilar. *Our Cry for Life: Feminist Theology from Latin America*. Maryknoll, NY: Orbis, 1993.

Augustine, Saint. *On Christian Doctrine*. Translated by D. W. Robertson. Upper Saddle River, NJ: Prentice Hall, 1958.

de Ávila, Teresa. *Life of St. Teresa*. Translated by J. M. Cohen. Harmondsworth, UK: Penguin, 1957.

Benedict XVI. *Spe Sav*. Encyclical Letter. Vatican: Libreria Editrice Vaticana, 2007.

_____. *The Yes of Jesus Christ—Spiritual Exercises in Faith, Hope and Love*. Translated by Robert Nowell. 1989. http://www.alisonmorgan.co.uk/Ratzinger%20 91.pdf.

Benjamin, Walter. *The Arcades Project*. Translated by Howard Eiland and Kevin McLaughlin (based on German volume edited by Rolf Tiedemann). Cambridge, MA: Belknap, 1999.

_____. *One-Way Street and Other Writings*. Translated by Edmund Jephcott. London: New Left, 1979.

_____. *Selected Writings: Volume 3 1935-1938*. Translated by Edmund Jephcott, Howard Eiland, et al. Edited by Howard Eiland and Michael W. Jennings. Cambridge, MA: Belknap, 2002.

_____. *Selected Writings: Volume 4 1938-1940*. Translated by Edmund Jephcott et al. Edited by Howard Eiland and Michael W. Jennings. Cambridge, MA: Belknap, 2003.

_____. "Thesis on the Philosophy of History." In *Illuminations*. Translated by Harry Zohn. Edited by Hannah Arendt. New York: Schocken, 1968 [1940].

Bhabha, Homi K. *The Location of Culture*. New York: Routledge, 1994.

Bonnie, Richard J. "Political Abuse of Psychiatry in the Soviet Union and in China: Complexities and Controversies." *Journal of the American Academy of Psychiatry and the Law* 30 (2002): 136–44.

Butler, Smedley D. *War Is a Racket: The Antiwar Classic by America's Most Decorated Soldier*. Los Angeles: Feral House, 1935.

The Center for Latin American Studies (CLAS). *In the Shadow of the Wall: Family Separation, Immigration Enforcement and Security*. Tucson: Arizona University Press, 2013.

Colebrook, Claire. "Toxic Feminism: Hope and Hopelessness after Feminism." In *Hope and Feminist Theory*. Edited by Rebecca Coleman and Debra Ferreday. New York: Routledge, 2011.

de la Cruz, Juan. "Ascent of Mount Carmel." In *John of the Cross Selected Writings*. Edited by Kieran Kavanaugh. New York: Paulist, 1987 [1618].

_____. "The Spiritual Canticle." In *John of the Cross Selected Writings*. Edited by Kieran Kavanaugh. New York: Paulist, 1987 [1578].

De La Torre, Miguel A. *Latina/o Social Ethics: Moving Beyond Eurocentric Moral Thinking*. Waco, TX: Baylor University Press, 2010.

_____. *The U.S. Immigration Crises: Toward an Ethics of Place*. Eugene, OR: Cascade, 2016.

De La Torre, Miguel A., and Albert Hernández. *The Quest for the Historical Satan*. Minneapolis: Fortress Press, 2011.

Deloria Jr., Vine. *God Is Red: A Native View of Religion*. Golden, CO: Fulcrum, 2003 [1973].

DeNavas-Walt, Carmen, Bernadette D. Proctor, and Jessica C. Smith. *Income, Poverty, and Health Insurance Coverage in the United States: 2010*. Washington, DC: U.S. Census Bureau, September 2011.

Dussel, Enrique. *Philosophy of Liberation*. Translated by Aquilina Martinez and Christine Morkovsky. Maryknoll, NY: Orbis, 1990.

_____. *The Postmodernism Debate in Latin America*. Edited by John Beverly, Michael Aronna, and José Oviedo. Durham, NC: Duke University Press, 1995.

Eagleton, Terry. *Hope without Optimism*. Charlottesville: University of Virginia Press, 2015.

Earle, Peter G. "Unamuno and the Theme of History." *Hispanic Review* 32, no. 4 (October 1964): 319–39.

Enright, Robert, and Richard Fitzgibbons. *Helping Clients Forgive: An Empirical Guide for Resolving Anger and Restoring Hope*. Washington, DC: American Psychological Association, 2000.

Fanon, Frantz. *The Wretched of the Earth.* Translated by Constance Farrington. New York: Grove, 1963.

Fitting, Elizabeth. *The Struggle for Maize: Campesinos, Workers, and Transgenic Corn in the Mexican Countryside.* Durham, NC: Duke University Press, 2011.

Freire, Paulo. *Pedagogy of the Oppressed.* Translated by Myra Bergman Ramos. New York: Continuum, 1994 [1968].

Floyd-Thomas, Stacey. *Deeper Shades of Purple: Womanism in Religion and Society.* New York: New York University Press, 2006.

Food and Agriculture Organization of the United Nations (FAO). *The State of Food Insecurity in the World, 2012.* Rome: Food and Agriculture Organization of the United Nations, 2012.

Foucault, Michel. *The Birth of the Clinic: An Archaeology of Medical Perception.* Translated by A. M. Sheridan. New York: Routledge, 1989 [1963].

_____. *Discipline and Punish: The Birth of the Prison.* Translated by Alan Sheridan. New York: Vintage, 1995 [1975].

_____. *The Foucault Reader.* Edited by Paul Rabino. New York: Pantheon, 1984.

_____. *Madness and Civilization: A History of Insanity in the Age of Reason.* Translated by Richard Howard. New York: Vintage, 1988 [1961].

_____. *Technologies of the Self: A Seminar with Michel Foucault.* Edited by Luther H. Martin, Huck Gutman, and Patrick H. Hutton. Amherst: University of Massachusetts Press, 1988.

Glenn, Jerome C., Theodore J. Gordon, and Elizabeth Florescu. *2012 State of the Future.* Washington, DC: The Millennium Project, 2012.

Goizueta, Roberto S. *Caminemos con Jesús: Toward a Hispanic/Latino Theology of Accompaniment.* Maryknoll, NY: Orbis, 1995.

Gushee, David. *The Future of Faith in American Politics: The Public Witness of the Evangelical Center.* Waco, TX: Baylor University Press, 2008.

Halaas, David Fridtjof, and Andrew E. Masich. *Halfbreed: The Remarkable True Story of George Bent—Caught Between the Worlds of the Indian and the White Man.* Cambridge, MA: Da Capo, 2004.

Hamber, Brandon. "Does the Truth Heal?: A Psychological Perspective on Political Strategies for Dealing with the Legacy of Political Violence." In *Burying the Past: Making Peace and Doing Justice after Civil Conflict.* Edited by Nigel Biggar. Washington, DC: Georgetown University Press, 2003.

Hassig, Ralph, and Kongdan Oh, *The Hidden People of North Korea: Everyday Life in the Hermit Kingdom.* Lanham, MD: Rowman & Littlefield, 2009.

Hegel, Georg Wilhelm Friedrich. *Aesthetics: Lectures on Fine Art.* Translated by T. M. Knox. Oxford: Oxford University Press, 1975 [1835].

_____. *Elements of the Philosophy of Right.* Translated by H. B. Nisbet. Edited by Allen W. Wood. Cambridge: Cambridge University Press, 1991 [1820].

_____. *Lectures on the Philosophy of World History.* Translated by H. B. Nisbet. Cambridge: Cambridge University Press, 1975 [1857].

_____. *The Philosophy of History.* Translated by J. Sibree. New York: Colonial, 1900 [1824].

_____. *Philosophy of the Mind.* Translated by William Wallace and A. V. Miller. Oxford: Oxford University Press, 2007 [1807].

Hernández, Albert. *Subversive Fire: The Untold Story of Pentecost.* Lexington, KY: Emeth Press, 2010.

Hoig, Stan. *The Sand Creek Massacre.* Norman, OK: University of Oklahoma Press, 1961.

Hoyt, Thomas. "Interpreting Biblical Scholarship for the Black Church Tradition." In *Stony the Road We Trod.* Edited by Cain Hope Felder. Minneapolis: Fortress Press, 1991.

Hyok Kang with Philippe Grangereau, *This Is Paradise!: My North Korean Childhood.* Translated by Shaun Whiteside. London: Little, Brown, 2004.

Jang Jin-Sung. *Dear Leader: My Escape from North Korea.* Translated by Shirley Lee. New York: Atria, 2014.

Jiangang Jiu, Jun Li, Ling Feng, Ling Li, and Jie Tian. "Seeing Jesus in Toast: Neural and Behavioral Correlates of Face Pareidolia," *Cortex* 53, no. 60 (April 2014): 60–77.

Justin Martyr. *St. Justin Martyr: The First and Second Apologies.* Translated by L. W. Barnard. Mahwah, NJ: Paulist, 1997.

Kant, Immanuel. *Foundations of the Metaphysics of Morals.* Translated by Lewis White Beck. New York: Liberal Arts, 1959 [1785].

Kee, Alistair. "The Criticism of [Black] Theology Is Transformed into the Criticism of Politics." In *The Quest for Liberation and Reconciliation: Essays in Honor of J. Deotis Roberts.* Edited by Michael Battle. Louisville: Westminster John Knox, 2005.

Kelman, Ari. *A Misplaced Massacre: Struggling over the Memory of Sand Creek.* Cambridge, MA: Harvard University Press, 2013.

Khatib, Sami. "The Messianic Without Messianism: Walter Benjamin's Materialist Theology." *Anthropology & Materialism: A Journal of Social Research* 1 (2003).

Kidwell, Clara Sue, Homer Noley, and George E. "Tink" Tinker. *A Native American Theology.* Maryknoll, NY: Orbis, 2001.

King Jr., Martin Luther. *A Testament of Hope: The Essential Writings and Speeches of Martin Luther King.* New York: HarperCollins, 1986.

Labor Council for Latin American Advancement (LCLAA). *Another America Is Possible: The Impact of NAFTA on the U.S. Latino Community and Lessons for Future*

Trade Agreements, Product ID 9013. Washington, DC: Public Citizen's Global Trade Watch, 2004.

Lacan, Jacques. *Écrits: A Selection*. Translated by Alan Sheridan. New York: W. W. Norton, 1977.

Laclau, Ernesto. "Politics and the Limits of Modernity." *Universal Abandon? The Politics of Postmodernism*. Edited by Andrew Ross. Minneapolis: University of Minnesota Press, 1988.

Lankov, Andrei. *North of the DMZ: Essays on Daily Life in North Korea*. Jefferson, NC: McFarland, 2007.

———. *The Real North Korea: Life and Politics in the Failed Stalinist Utopia*. New York: Oxford University Press, 2013.

Lederach, John Paul. *Building Peace: Sustainable Reconciliation in Divided Societies*. Washington, DC: U.S. Institute of Peace, 1997.

———. *The Journey toward Reconciliation*. Waterloo, ON: Herald, 1999.

Marsden, George M. *Fundamentalism and American Culture: The Shaping of Twentieth-Century Evangelism 1870–1925*. New York: Oxford University Press, 1980.

Martí, José. *Our America by José Martí: Writings on Latin America and the Struggle for Cuban Independence*. Edited by Philip S. Foner. Translated by Elinor Randall, Juan de Onís, and Roslyn Held Foner. New York: Monthly Review, 1977 [1889].

Martin, Bradley K. *Under the Loving Care of the Fatherly Leader: North Korea and the Kim Dynasty*. New York: St. Martin's, 2004.

McAfee Brown, Robert. "Introduction." *The Trial of God: As It Was Held on February 25, 1649, in Shamgorod*. New York: Schocken, 1995.

Moltmann, Jürgen. *Ethics of Hope*. Translated by Margaret Kohl. Minneapolis: Fortress Press, 2012.

———. *God in Creation: A New Theology of Creation and the Spirit of God*. Translated by Margaret Kohl. Minneapolis: Fortress Press, 1993 [1985].

———. *Hope and Planning*. Translated by Margaret Clarkson. London: SCM, 1971.

———. *The Living God and the Fullness of Life*. Translated by Margaret Kohl. Geneva: World Council of Churches, 2016.

———. *Man: Christian Anthropology in the Conflicts of the Present*. Translated by John Sturdy. London: SPCK, 1974.

———. *On Human Dignity: Political Theology and Ethics*. Translated by M. Douglas Meeks. Philadelphia: Fortress Press, 1984.

———. *Religion, Revolution and the Future*. Translated by M. Douglas Meeks. New York: Scribner's, 1969.

———. *Theology of Hope: On the Ground and the Implications of a Christian Eschatology*. Translated by James W. Leitch. New York: Harper & Row, 1967.

Nietzsche, Friedrich. *The Gay Science.* Translated by Josefine Nauckoff. Edited by Bernard Williams. Cambridge: Cambridge University Press, 2001 [1882].

———. *The Genealogy of Morals.* Translated by Walter Kaufmann and R. J. Hollingdale. New York: Vintage, 1989 [1887].

Nishida Kitaro. *Last Writings: Nothingness and the Religious Worldview.* Translated by David A. Dilworth. Honolulu: University of Hawaii Press, 1987.

No More Deaths. *A Culture of Cruelty: Abuse and Impunity in Short-Term U.S. Border Patrol Custody* (Tucson, AZ: No More Deaths, 2011).

Ortiz, Fernando. *Contrapunteo cubano del tabaco y el azúcar.* La Habana: Dirección de Publicaciones Universidad Central de Las Villas, 1963.

O'Sullivan, John. "Annexation." *United States Magazine and Democratic Review* 17, no. 1 (July and August 1845): 5–10.

Pérez, Louis A. Jr. *Essays on Cuban History: Historiography and Research.* Gainesville: University Press of Florida, 1995.

Rhodes, Richard. "The General and World War III." *The New Yorker* 71, no. 17 (June 19, 1995): 47–59.

Rauschenbusch, Walter. *Christianity and the Social Crisis.* Louisville: Westminster John Knox, 1991 [1907].

Said, Edward. *Culture and Imperialism.* New York: Alfred A. Knopf, 1993.

Salcedo, Emilio. "Unamuno y Ortega Y Gasset: Dialogo entre dos españoles." In *Cuadernos de la cátedra Miguel de Unamuno.* Salamanca: n.a., 1956.

Segundo, Juan Luis. *Signs of the Times: Theological Reflections.* Translated by Robert R. Barr. Maryknoll, NY: Orbis, 1993.

Selden, Mark. "A Forgotten Holocaust: US Bombing Strategy, the Destruction of Japanese Cities and the American Way of War from World War II to Iraq." *The Asia-Pacific Journal* 5, no. 5 (May 2, 2007).

Scaer, David P. "Jürgen Moltmann and His Theology of Hope." *Journal of the Evangelical Theological Society* 12, no. 2 (1970): 69–79.

Scott, James C. *Domination and the Arts of Resistance: Hidden Transcripts.* New Haven: Yale University Press, 1990.

Smith, Robert F. *What Happened in Cuba? A Documentary History.* New York: Twayne, 1963.

Stana, Richard M. *INS' Southwest Border Strategy: Resource and Impact Issues Remain After Seven Years.* Washington, DC: U.S. General Accounting Office, 2001.

Striffler, Steve, and Mark Moberg, eds. *Banana Wars: Power, Production, and History in the Americas.* Durham, NC: Duke University Press, 2003.

Takaki, Ronald. *A Different Mirror: A History of Multicultural America.* Boston: Little, Brown, 1993.

Tinker, George E. "Redskin, Tanned Hide: A Book of Christian History Bound in the Flayed Skin of an American Indian." *Journal of Race, Ethnicity, and Religion* 5, no. 9 (October 2014): 1–43.

_____. "Tink." *Missionary Conquest: The Gospel and Native American Cultural Genocide*. Minneapolis: Fortress Press, 1993.

Thomas, Hugh. *Cuba: The Pursuit of Freedom*. New York: Harper & Row, 1971.

Tuhiwai Smith, Linda. London: Zed Books, 2012. *Decolonizing Methodologies: Research and Indigenous Peoples*, 2nd ed.

Yeonmi Park (with Maryanne Vollers). *In Order to Live: A North Korean Girl's Journey to Freedom*. New York: Pilgrim, 2015.

Salcedo, Emilio. "Unamuno y Ortega Y Gasset: Dialogo entre dos españoles." In *Cuadernos de la cátedra Miguel de Unamuno*. Salamanca: n.a., 1956.

de Unamuno, Miguel. "Arbitrary Reflections upon Europeanization." In *Essays and Soliloquies*. Translated by John Ernest Crawford Flitch. New York: Alfred A. Knopf, 1925.

_____. "Del sentimiento trágico de la vida." In *Filosofia*. Madrid: Akal Ediciones, 1996 [1912].

_____. *Diario Intimo*. Edited by Etelvino González López. Salamanca: Ediciones Universidad de Salamanca, 2012 [1897].

_____. *El Cristo de Velázquez*. Madrid: Espasa Calpe, 1920.

_____. "En torno al casticismo." In *Obras completes: Ensayos, Vol VIII*. Edited by Ricardo Senabre, pp. 59–199. Madrid: Fundación José Antonio de Castro, 2007 [1895].

_____. "La fe." In *Tres Ensayos*. Edited by B Rodríguez Serra, pp. 45–70. Madrid: Imprenta de A. Marzo, 1900.

_____. "La oración del ateo." In *Obras complete*, vol. 6. Edited by Manuel García Blanco, p. 359. Madrid: Escelicer, 1966 [1910].

_____. "The Life of Don Quixote and Sancho." In *Selected Works of Miguel de Unamuno, Volume 3: Our Lord Don Quixote*. Translated by Anthony Kerrigan, pp. 23–329. Princeton: Princeton University Press, 1967 [1905].

_____. "Mi religion." In *Unamuno, Azorin y Ortega: Ensayos*. Edited by Ernesto Livacic Gazzano, pp. 49–56. Santiago, Chile: Editorial Andres Bello, 1978 [1907].

United Nations Development Programme (UNDP). *Fighting Climate Change: Human Solidarity in a Divided World*. New York: Palgrave Macmillan, 2007.

_____. *The Real Wealth of Nations: Pathways to Human Development*. New York: Palgrave Macmillan, 2010.

Walker, Alice. *In Search of Our Mothers' Gardens*. London: Women's Press, 1984.

Warrior, Robert Allen, "Canaanites, Cowboys, and Indians." In *Christianity and Crises* in *Ethics in the Present Tense: Readings from Christianity and Crises*

1966-1991. Edited by Leon Howell and Vivian Lindermayer. New York: Friendship, 1991.

Wiesel, Elie. *The Trial of God: As It Was Held on February 25, 1649, in Shamgorod*. New York: Schocken, 1995 [1979].

Winant, Howard. *The New Politics of Race: Globalism, Difference, Justice*. Minneapolis: University of Minnesota Press, 2004.

Index of Names and Subjects

Lightning Source UK Ltd.
Milton Keynes UK
UKHW020624230222
399111UK00006B/237